Best Wishes

Relish
SOUTH WEST

Original recipes from the South West's
finest chefs and restaurants.
Introduction by Michael Caines MBE.

First Published 2013
By Relish Publications
Shield Green Farm, Tritlington,
Northumberland, NE61 3DX.

ISBN: 978-0-9575370-4-0

Publisher: Duncan L Peters
General Manager: Teresa Peters
Design: Vicki Brown
Relish Photography: Andy Richardson
www.awaywithmedia.com Twitter: @andyrichardson1
Editorial Consultant: Paul Robertson
The Relish Team: Valerie McLeod, Wendy Rutterford,
Gillian Scribbins

Front cover: Allium Brasserie by Andy Richardson

Printed in Slovenia on behalf of Latitude Press

Relish
PUBLICATIONS

Relish
OUR HAND PICKED RESTAURANTS

As the proud owner of a Relish cookbook, you may subscribe for your own personal Relish Rewards card which entitles you to free membership for one year.

You can access the Relish members' area on our website and find out what exclusive offers are available to you from the fantastic restaurants featured in our series of books throughout the UK.

SUBSCRIBE FOR YOUR REWARD CARD ON OUR HOMEPAGE
Simply register your name, address and title of Relish book purchased to receive your **FREE Relish Reward Card** - www.relishpublications.co.uk/relish-rewards

When you book, just let the restaurant know that you are a member and take your card along with you.

WHAT ARE THE REWARDS?
The rewards will continue to be updated on the website so do check and keep in touch. These range from a free bottle of Champagne to free gifts when you dine. Relish will send you a quarterly newsletter with special discounts, rewards and free recipes. We are about quality not quantity!

All offers are subject to change. See the Relish website for details.

www.relishpublications.co.uk

004
CONTENTS

DESSERTS

006
CONTENTS

DESSERTS

RESTAURANTS

INTRODUCTION BY MICHAEL CAINES

Cooking is my passion. I can't imagine life outside the kitchen. My interest in food began when I was a child, although I always thought I would have a career in the military, not as a chef! Growing up as one of six children, meal times were a busy family event around the table, enjoying fruit and vegetables grown by dad and turned into wonderful simple meals by my mum, with a little help from me. It was a last minute decision to train as a chef and I have never looked back.

I started my career at Exeter Catering College, where I now have my own Academy, before going on to work at The Grosvenor House Hotel in London. I had the opportunity to work for Raymond Blanc and the late Bernard Loiseau, two of my culinary heroes. Raymond put me forward for the role at Gidleigh Park where I have spent the past 19 years, achieved two Michelin stars and five AA rosettes. It feels like only yesterday that I took up the helm, but time flies when you are enjoying yourself.

As a Devon boy I have always felt the importance of supporting local producers; in a rural area it helps small communities to thrive and keeps businesses and families in the region. For me, it means that I always have great produce to inspire my menus. The south west continues to lead the UK in high quality, authentic cooking with locally sourced ingredients and that's what makes it special.

But don't just take my word for it! This book is packed full of exceptional places to eat, and delicious recipes to cook, so get stuck into it and hopefully the south west will inspire you as much as it inspires me.

Michael Caines MBE
Food and Beverage Director at Brownsword
Hotels and Executive Chef at Gidleigh Park

010
ABODE EXETER

Cathedral Yard, Exeter, Devon, EX1 1HD

01392 319 955
www.abodeexeter.co.uk

Centrally located in the heart of Exeter's beautiful Cathedral Yard, this hotel has a rich history. Formerly the historic Royal Clarence Hotel, the establishment is reported to be the first hotel in England. ABode Exeter has continued to build upon a tradition of excellence and quality to create the city's most exciting venue, and Michael Caines' Restaurant at ABode Exeter, overlooking the beautiful Cathedral Green, is Exeter's most fabulous place to dine.

Exeter is home to two Michelin-starred chef Michael Caines MBE and, fittingly, Michael has overseen the restaurant since 2000 with the help of head chef Ian Webber. Together they have been serving guests, food critics and friends an interpretation of Michael's highly individual and acclaimed style of cuisine, pioneered at nearby Gidleigh Park and utilising the finest produce from the West Country.

The hotel itself offers individual, contemporary design allied with tradition and understated elegance. Bedrooms have been designed with a sense of luxury and relaxation so guests can enjoy an ideal night's sleep, and wake up refreshed and rejuvenated. With the temptations of exceptional dining and fine wine paired with elegant bedrooms, it's easy to see why ABode Exeter and the Michael Caines' Restaurant are amongst Exeter's most popular venues.

Relish Restaurant Rewards
See page 003 for details.

Located in the stunning Cathedral Yard, Michael Caines'
Restaurant at ABode Exeter has become one of the
city's finest places to dine under the expert guidance
of Michael Caines and head chef Ian Webber.

SALT COD, BRIXHAM CRAB, LEMON & CHORIZO SALAD

SERVES 4

Trimbach, Pinot Blanc 2010 Alsace
(France)

Ingredients

240g cod or pollock fillet
(salted, dusted with smoked paprika)

Lemon Purée

10 lemons (peel and juice of)
2 x 15g sugar
2 x 5g salt
5g turmeric
10ml sugar syrup (see page 231)

Brixham Crab

100g white crabmeat
(bound with a little mayonnaise)
50g brown crabmeat
(mixed with 25g mayonnaise)

Garnish

4 small chorizo sausages
mixed salad and sorrel leaves
olive oil and lemon juice (to dress)
40g samphire
(*blanched* in boiling water and refreshed)
4 lemon segments (cut into triangles)

Method

For The Lemon Purée

Blanch the lemon peel 10 times in boiling water with 15g of sugar and 5g of salt each time, using the 5g of turmeric for the first *blanch* only. There's no reason why the same water can't be used for *blanch* number 2-10, as long as it is brought to the boil and the lemon peel is removed and plunged into cold water each time. Blend with the sugar syrup and fresh lemon juice, adjusting the flavour with the syrup, lemon juice and salt, as required.

For The Fish

Gently cook the fish for 12 minutes at 55°C (see chef's tip) or poach gently in olive oil and herbs.

> **Chef's Tip**
>
> In the restaurant we use a water bath and vacuum pack the fish, but at home you could use a nice olive oil scented with lemon zest and fresh herbs.

To Serve

Grill the chorizo.

Carefully dress the salad leaves, then arrange all the ingredients on the plate as you wish.

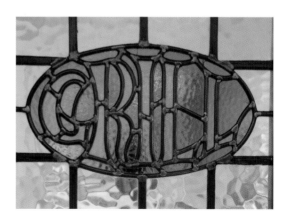

(see glossary)

DUCK, HARICOT BEAN & FENNEL CASSOULET, FIVE SPICE SAUCE

SERVES 4

 Seresin Momo, Pinot Noir 2010 Marlborough (New Zealand)

Ingredients

Duck

1-2 ducks
(depending on size and how hungry you are!)
sea salt
duck fat (to cover)

Haricot Beans

200g white haricot beans
(soaked overnight if using dried)
200ml chicken stock
1 bouquet garni
50g carrot (roughly chopped)
1 onion (roughly chopped)

Cassoulet

4 bulbs fennel (braised in 500ml chicken stock)
60g fennel (diced)
60g lardons (cooked in oil)
2 sprigs tarragon (leaves picked and chopped)
olive oil
10g butter

Duck And Five Spice Sauce

2 onions (cut into rings)
1 sprig tarragon
2 sprigs thyme
5g five spice (to dust)
500ml chicken stock
250ml basic veal glaze
100ml honey
50ml sherry vinegar
100ml double cream

Garnish

fennel fronds

Chef's Tip

Duck fat can be purchased from most supermarkets. Alternatively, ask your butcher for duck skin and render it in a low oven.

Method

Ask your butcher to bone the ducks and chop the bones for you.

For The Duck Confit (Prepare the day before)

Salt the duck legs for 12 hours, wash, then cook in the liquid duck fat for 2-4 hours at 120-140°C or until the meat is falling from the bone. Cool in the fat. Pick the meat from the bone.

For The Haricot Beans

Place all the ingredients in a large pan, bring to the boil, then simmer until the beans are tender, for approximately 1 hour.

For The Fennel

Preheat the oven to 180°C. Braise the fennel bulbs (but not the separate 60g of diced fennel) in the chicken stock, on the hob, for 15 minutes. Drain, reserving the stock. Blend 2 of the bulbs to a purée in a liquidiser using some of the reserved chicken stock to loosen if required, then cut the other 2 bulbs in half, drizzle with olive oil and roast in the oven for 20 minutes.

For The Duck And Five Spice Sauce

Preheat the oven to 175°C. Roast the duck bones with the onion, thyme and tarragon for 15-25 minutes until lightly coloured. Dust with the five spice, then cook for a further 5 minutes.

Add the bones to a saucepan, cover with chicken stock and basic veal glaze.

Simmer the honey in a separate saucepan until it turns amber. Add the sherry vinegar and bring to a simmer, then reduce until the flavour is balanced between sweet and sour. Add to your sauce along with the double cream. Simmer for 1-1¼ hours, pass through a fine sieve or cheese cloth and then reduce until the sauce coats the back of a spoon.

For The Cassoulet

Blend one third of the haricot bean mixture to a purée, then mix with the roasted fennel and fennel purée, lardons, remaining haricot beans, chopped tarragon, confit duck and duck sauce. Cover and leave in a warm place. Roast the diced fennel in olive oil and butter until golden. Heat the cassoulet and fold the ingredients together then plate as you wish.

For The Duck Breast

Score the duck breast on its skin, pan roast until the skin is crisp, turn briefly and continue to cook to your taste. Allow to rest for 5-10 minutes.

To Serve

Slice the duck breast and plate with the cassoulet. Garnish with fennel fronds.

THYME ROASTED PLUMS, VANILLA RICE PUDDING, SPICED PLUM SORBET

SERVES 4

 Contero Moscato d'Asti di Strevi DOCG 2012
Piemonte (Italy)

Ingredients

Rice Pudding

240g pudding rice
1 litre full-fat milk
1 litre double cream
1 vanilla pod (split lengthways)
150g caster sugar

Sorbet

1.4kg plums
400g caster sugar
400ml water
1 stick cinnamon
2 cloves
1 blade mace
10 black peppercorns
1 star anise
1 vanilla pod (split lengthways)

Roast Plums

8 plums
2 sprigs thyme (picked)
60g Demerara sugar

Method

For The Rice Pudding

Blanch the rice for 3 minutes and drain. Put the milk, cream, sugar and vanilla into a large pan then add the rice. Bring to the boil, reduce the heat and cook on the stove for 30 minutes, or bake in an ovenproof dish at 140ºC for 30-40 minutes.

For The Sorbet (Prepare the day before)

Make a stock syrup from the sugar and water (see page 231). Add the spices and plums, then poach until soft. Leave overnight to infuse. Remove the stones from the plums and the whole spices, then blend in a liquidiser. Churn in an ice cream machine and keep in the freezer.

> **Chef's Tip**
>
> If you don't have an ice cream machine, then the sorbet mix can be frozen in a tray and scraped with a fork into a granita, and served on the side in a glass.

For The Roast Plums

Preheat the oven to 200ºC. Remove the stones from the plums, then sprinkle with the picked thyme and 10g of the sugar. Roast in the oven for 10-12 minutes until the plums are soft and the juices and sugar have turned into a syrup.

At the same time, on a non-stick tray, sprinkle the 50g of Demerara sugar and cook until caramelised, for approximately 15-20 minutes. Remove from the oven and allow to cool.

To Serve

Spoon the rice onto the plate and arrange the plums and their cooking juices over and around. *Quenelle* the sorbet and serve on the side. Scatter over the caramelised Demerara sugar.

020
ALLIUM BRASSERIE

Abbey Hotel, North Parade, Bath, Somerset, BA1 1LF

01225 461 603
www.abbeyhotelbath.co.uk

Chris Staines has been something of a whirlwind in the industry. As a mere youngster he was head chef at Foliage, Mandarin Oriental, London, where he held a Michelin star for seven years and before that he was chef de cuisine at Marco Pierre White's The Oak Room, which held three Michelin stars at the time - an impressive start to his career in some of the country's toughest kitchens. Chris is today one of the UK's most acclaimed chefs, highly regarded by his peers and with an ever growing fan base amongst the south west's serious foodies. In only 18 months he has established Allium as a must visit restaurant in Bath.

Chris has a no nonsense philosophy when it comes to his style of cooking. "People like to pigeon-hole restaurants," he says, "because it makes it easier to define them, but I am simply sourcing the best ingredients I can find, combining that with a high skill level in the kitchen, and producing dishes of variety and style."

"Allium is the kind of restaurant that we would all love to have nearby; the ambience is relaxed and welcoming, there is a great wine list to match the food and the menu changes frequently. You are just as welcome to order a couple of things from the snack menu, with a great glass of wine, as you are to linger all day."
Chris Staines, Chef Patron

Relish Restaurant Rewards
See page 003 for details.

In 18 months Chris has created something special with Allium Brasserie, formerly the Bath Tea Rooms. An interior refurbishment was undertaken and Allium version one was launched. Chris has a clear vision for Allium; a restaurant for locals, great food, well cooked, well priced. With a skilled team supporting him, Chris has carved out a niche in the Bath restaurant scene.

They have already earned three AA rosettes in recognition of the hard work they have put in, and Allium will grow and evolve in the coming years. This is just the start.

LIGHTLY CURED SMOKED SALMON, POACHED OYSTERS, CUCUMBER & VERBENA GAZPACHO

SERVES 4

 Black Label Grüner Veltliner, Yealands (New Zealand)

Ingredients

8 fresh oysters (shelled, cleaned, juice reserved)

Salmon

250g salmon fillet
50g salt
50g sugar
1 lemon (zest of)
olive oil (to cover)

Cucumber And Verbena Gazpacho

240g cucumber (roughly chopped)
26g celery (roughly chopped)
4g mint (chopped)
7g lemon verbena (chopped)
salt (pinch of)
sugar (pinch of)
cayenne pepper (pinch of)
80g crème fraîche
12ml lime juice

Fresh Vegetables

1 stick celery (peeled and sliced)
2 Granny Smith apples (peeled, cut into 2½cm batons)

Oyster Mayonnaise

2 raw oysters
1 tbsp English mustard
1 tbsp white wine vinegar
150ml vegetable oil
1 lemon (juice of)
salt (to taste)

Garnish

fennel fronds, borage flowers, coriander leaf (picked)

Method

For The Cucumber And Verbena Gazpacho (Prepare the day before)

Mix together the cucumber, celery, mint and verbena in a non-reactive container. Season with a pinch of salt, sugar and cayenne pepper. Leave to marinate overnight.

The next day, place the marinated vegetables into a food processor with the crème fraîche and slowly add the lime juice. Blend the soup until smooth, then pass through a fine sieve. Check the seasoning and adjust as necessary. Refrigerate until needed.

For The Cured Smoked Salmon

Cut the salmon into 50-60g portions. Mix the salt, sugar and lemon zest and sprinkle over the salmon, liberally. Leave for an hour, then wash the salmon under cold running water.

Now lightly smoke the salmon using a food smoker. We use hickory wood to give the salmon a unique smoky flavour, or you may buy lightly smoked salmon from the supermarket.

Gently heat the olive oil (enough to just cover the salmon) to 42°C, remove from the heat and drop the salmon into the oil for 20 minutes. Reserve in the fridge until required.

For The Oyster Mayonnaise

Gently open the oysters and place the meat and strained juice in a food processor along with the mustard and white wine vinegar. Slowly start adding the vegetable oil, blending all the time to form a mayonnaise. Add a few drops of lemon juice and reserve in the fridge to set.

To Serve

Pipe some of the oyster mayonnaise into the bottom of your serving bowl and arrange the salmon on top. Meanwhile, lightly heat your oysters in a small saucepan in their own juices until just warm. Place the oysters in the bowl along with the apple batons and celery.

Sprinkle the picked herbs on top of the salmon. Serve the cucumber gazpacho in a small jug on the side.

Chef's Tip

You can prepare all the elements of this recipe a day or two in advance and then assemble the dish just before serving.

CORNISH HAKE, THAI SPICED BUTTERNUT SQUASH, PRAWNS, PEANUT & TAMARIND JAM, CITRUS DRESSING

SERVES 4

 Riesling Trimbach
(France)

Ingredients

4 x 160g hake (lightly seasoned with salt)
12 tiger prawns (peeled, shells reserved for the sauce)

Citrus Dressing
2 pink grapefruit, 2 large oranges
200ml stock syrup (see page 231)
1 lemon (squeeze of, optional)

Peanut And Tamarind Jam
10g ginger (finely chopped)
½ tsp garlic (minced)
½ red chilli (finely chopped)
1½ dried chillies (deep fried, finely chopped)
10g dried shrimp
50g palm sugar (grated)
65ml water
30ml soy sauce, 15ml fish sauce
100g roasted peanuts (chopped)
24ml tamarind water
25g shallots (deep fried, finely chopped)
1 lime (zest and juice of)

Thai Spiced Butternut Sauce
shells and heads from the 12 prawns
4 sticks lemongrass
4 kaffir lime leaves
1 red chilli (chopped)
20g ginger (finely chopped)
2 shallots (finely sliced), 2 cloves garlic (crushed)
300ml coconut milk
200g butternut squash (chopped)
10ml fish sauce, 1 lime (juice of)

To Serve
pak choi, butternut squash dice, spring onions
(chopped, stir fried)

Garnish
fresh coriander, cress, shiso leaves

Method

For The Thai Spiced Butternut Sauce
Place the lemongrass, lime leaves, chilli, ginger, shallots and garlic into a pestle and mortar or food processor and pulse to a fine paste.

Add 2 tablespoons of coconut milk into a heavy-bottomed saucepan or wok and fry until the oil splits from the milk. Add the spice paste and fry gently until fragrant. Add the prawn shells to the pan, then fry again until fragrant.

Cover with the remaining coconut milk and cook gently for 10 minutes. Strain the liquid, discard the paste and shells. Return the stock to the pan, then add the butternut squash. Bring to the boil and simmer gently until the butternut is soft. Place the sauce into a food processor and blend to a smooth sauce-like consistency, strain through a fine sieve. Add lime juice and fish sauce to taste.

For The Peanut And Tamarind Jam
Gently fry the garlic, ginger, chilli and shrimp in 2 tablespoons of vegetable oil until fragrant. Add the palm sugar and cook gently until caramelised. Add the soy sauce, fish sauce and water and bring to the boil. Add the peanuts, zest, tamarind water and fried shallots. Cook until the jam becomes sticky, stirring constantly. Remove from the heat, season with the lime juice.

For The Citrus Dressing
Cut the zest of the grapefruit and oranges into small dice, place in a pan of cold water and bring to the boil. Drain and repeat this process 3 times until the zest is soft.

Remove the pith from the fruit. Cut out the segments, then cut the flesh into small pieces and mix this with the zest.

Make a stock syrup with the sugar and water. Leave to cool. Mix in the fruit, taste, and adjust with a squeeze of lemon if necessary (optional depending upon your taste).

For The Hake And Prawns
Seal the hake in a small vacuum pack bag and place into a water bath at 55°C for 15 minutes or until soft to the touch. Seal the prawns in vacuum bags and add to the water bath with the hake for the last 3 minutes. Alternatively you could panfry the hake for 6 minutes or until a toothpick enters the flesh with no resistance and the prawns just before serving.

To Serve
Lay a fillet of hake in a bowl over the stir fried vegetables and spoon over the citrus dressing. Divide the prawns between the bowls, spoon the heated Thai sauce liberally into each bowl and top with a tablespoon of peanut and tamarind jam. Garnish with a sprinkling of coriander, cress and shiso leaves.

LIGHTLY POACHED PEACHES WITH ENGLISH RASPBERRIES, LEMON VERBENA ICE CREAM & A TARRAGON SYRUP

SERVES 4

 Cattunar Muscat, Istra (Croatia)

Ingredients

Peaches

2 or 3 large peaches
1 sprig lemon thyme (or thyme)
100g sugar
300ml water
½ vanilla pod (or 1 tsp vanilla extract)

Raspberry Purée

225g raspberries
2 tbsp icing sugar

Tarragon Syrup

bunch tarragon (picked)
100g caster sugar
100ml water

Lemon Verbena Ice Cream

200ml full-fat milk
70ml double cream
55g sugar
14g atomised glucose
20g milk powder (or non-fat milk solids)
2 egg yolks
15g lemon verbena leaves

Garnish

1 punnet fresh English raspberries
sugared almonds
biscotti (crumbed)
tarragon leaves (picked)

Method

For The Tarragon Syrup

Boil the sugar and water together to form a light syrup, place in a food processor and add the tarragon leaves. Blend until a smooth vibrant green syrup is achieved. Pass the syrup through a fine sieve and cool quickly to stop the syrup going brown.

For The Raspberry Purée

Simply blend the raspberries with the icing sugar to make a purée.

For The Poached Peaches

Peel the peaches and cut into nice wedge shaped pieces, allowing 5 or 6 wedges per person. Meanwhile, bring to the boil the sugar, water, thyme and vanilla in a pan. Remove from the heat, add the peach segments to the poaching liquor and allow to cool.

For The Lemon Verbena Ice Cream (Prepare the day before)

Mix the egg yolks, sugar, atomised glucose and milk powder to a paste. Meanwhile, in a heavy-bottomed saucepan, boil the milk and cream with the lemon verbena. Once boiled, pour the hot liquid over your paste and mix well. Return the mixture to your saucepan on a low heat, stirring continuously until the mix starts to thicken (83°C) and coats the back of a spoon. Cool rapidly to stop the eggs cooking further. Leave overnight in the fridge for the flavours to infuse and mature, then churn in an ice cream machine, or see page 231.

To Assemble

Pipe a few blobs of raspberry purée onto your serving plate. Drain the peaches and scatter over the plate. Sprinkle over some of the biscotti crumb and sugared almonds. Add a few picked tarragon leaves to each plate and drizzle over some of the tarragon syrup. Finally, place a generous scoop of the lemon verbena ice cream onto each dish and serve.

> **Chef's Tip**
>
> Finish with biscotti crumb for added texture. Buy a good quality version or, better still, make your own.

030
AN BOESTI
AT ST MELLION INTERNATIONAL RESORT

Saltash, Plymouth, Cornwall, PL12 6SD

Tel 01579 351 351
www.st-mellion.co.uk

Our superb two AA rosette restaurant, An Boesti, is steeped in locality, using the very best of our local Cornish ingredients, and is the perfect location for romance, celebrations and all types of gatherings.

You will instantly feel relaxed as you enter this cool, contemporary restaurant. Our team will be ready to serve you a drink from a vast selection in our cocktail bar, or you could add some sparkle to your evening by choosing a bottle from our extensive Champagne list.

Immerse yourself in the soothing atmosphere and enjoy our award-winning, contemporary, cosmopolitan cuisine, which embraces the old concepts devised by Escoffier, and enhances them using modern techniques. The food shows great flair and imagination, using the very finest ingredients which are carefully selected with our local partners; all of which combine to create delicious flavoursome dishes with a wonderful balance and depth of flavour.

The wine list offers superb quality and value, favouring the more boutique vineyards and wineries as well as ensuring the cellar is well stocked with some traditional favourites.

Our wine dinners are renowned, held throughout the year and supported by the winemakers themselves.

Sure An Boesti is our posh restaurant, but at St Mellion we are diligently relaxed and unstuffy, and the dress code is distinctly informal - even the lobsters don't wear tails!

Relish Restaurant Rewards
See page 003 for details.

We take great pride and pleasure in using the very best ingredients from our local area; whether it is the humble potato from Dupath, the meats sourced from Scorrier near Redruth, the lamb from Launceston, the fish from Dartmouth or the fresh fruit and vegetables from within the Tamar Valley. To complement this, we offer the best Cornish wines from Camel Valley, the best ales from Sharp's Brewery and ciders from Cornish Orchard.

CORNISH GOAT'S CHEESE, TEXTURES OF FENNEL & ORANGE

SERVES 12

 Cailbourdin Pouilly-Fumé, Les Cornets, Loire Valley, 2011 (France)

Ingredients

Goat's Cheese Mousse

500g goat's cheese (Cornish preferably, rind removed)
125g water (boiling)
2 leaves bronze gelatine or vegetarian (soaked in cold water for a couple of minutes)

Fennel Crumb

5 tbsp Panko breadcrumbs (or regular breadcrumbs)
1 tbsp fennel seeds (blitzed)
½ tbsp table salt
10ml vegetable oil

Orange Gel

600ml pure orange juice (no bits)
6g agar agar

Fennel Crisp

1 fennel top (bright green part only, finely sliced)
100ml stock syrup (see page 231)

Fennel Jelly

6 bulbs fennel
18g Vegetal powder (similar to agar agar)

Dry Orange Garnish

1 orange (skinned and segmented)

Garnish

fennel fronds

Method

For The Goat's Cheese Mousse
Pour the boiling water into a blender with the soaked gelatine. Add the goat's cheese and blitz until smooth and silky. Spread evenly on a sheet of clingfilm, and roll into 2.5cm circumference rolls. Chill, or freeze if prepared in advance.

> **Chef's Tip**
> Alternatively, the goat's cheese mousse may be served as a canape, or is delicious on freshly toasted bread.

For The Fennel Crumb
Heat the oil up to 160ºC in a small pan, then add the breadcrumbs and fry until golden brown. Once golden, remove from the oil and drain on a cloth or a tea towel, making sure the crumb is not sitting in the drained oil. Put the crumbs into a bowl, add the fennel seeds and the table salt, mix together well and keep aside.

For The Orange Gel
Mix the agar with the orange juice. Bring to the boil then remove from the heat. Skim the impurities from the surface with a dessert spoon. Pour the mixture into any container that will fit into your fridge. Allow to cool down on a work surface, then place in fridge for 2-4 hours, until the mixture has set into a solid block. Blitz the set block until a smooth gel forms. Pass through a sieve to remove any lumps. Refrigerate for a further hour.

For The Fennel Crisp (Prepare the day before)
Bring the stock syrup to a rapid boil, add the fennel and cook until transparent, approximately 2-3 minutes. Carefully remove the fennel from the liquid and spread out on a baking tray lined with greaseproof paper. Cover with clingfilm and leave overnight.

For The Fennel Jelly
Liquidise the fennel, adding water if necessary, until smooth. Pour through a fine sieve. Measure 260ml of fennel juice into a cold pan. Add the Vegetal powder and whisk it into the fennel juice. Bring to the boil, whisking occasionally. Once boiled, skim the impurities from the surface. While still piping hot, pour quickly onto a non-stick tray, evening it out by tilting the tray. You will need to work quickly as it will set in a matter of seconds. Leave to cool. Once cool, wrap around the goat's cheese mousse as pictured.

For The Dry Orange Garnish (Prepare 24 hours in advance)
Cut the segments into quarters, lay on a tray and allow to air dry on a kitchen side, under an umbrella cake cover, for 24 hours.

To Serve
Serve as pictured.

TRIO OF CORNISH FISH, BOUILLABAISSE SAUCE, SAFFRON POTATO, SPRING ONION, MELON & CHERRY TOMATO

SERVES 10

 Reichsgraf von Kesselstatt Riesling 2010, Trier (Germany)

Ingredients

Monkfish, Red Mullet And Hake

500g monkfish (skin on)
500g red mullet (skin on, pin-boned)
500g hake (skin on, pin-boned)
100ml vegetable oil
250g butter

Saffron Potatoes

5 large baking potatoes (peeled)
1 tsp saffron
1 tbsp unsalted butter
250ml water (boiling)
1 tbsp vegetable stock

Air-Dried Tomatoes

30 cherry tomatoes
1 litre boiling water
1 litre iced water
1 tbsp oil
2 tbsp sugar
2 tbsp salt

Bouillabaisse

125ml olive oil
1 bulb fennel (roughly chopped)
3 red peppers (roughly chopped)
2 cloves garlic (roughly chopped)
50g tomato purée
1½ litres fish stock
6 plum tomatoes (roughly chopped)
1 tsp saffron
25g unsalted butter
125ml double cream
25ml lemon juice

Garnish

melon
spring onion

Method

For The Fish

Gently heat the oil and butter in a large pan, but do not allow the butter to burn. Place all the fish, skin-side down, into the pan. Remove the red mullet after 90 seconds, making sure the fish is cooked thoroughly. Remove the hake and monkfish 30 seconds later. Place on a dry cloth to absorb the butter and oil. Serve immediately.

For The Saffron Potatoes

Cut the potatoes into 2cm cubes to achieve the shape desired for a clean presentation. Place the saffron, butter, water and vegetable stock into a suitable pan and mix well, then add the potatoes. Simmer for 20-30 minutes or until the potatoes are soft. Strain and serve.

For The Air-Dried Tomatoes

Score the cherry tomatoes with a cross on the bottom. Place into rapidly boiling water until the skin starts to peel away. Remove from the boiling water and shock in iced water until cold. Once cold, carefully remove the skins. Cut the tomatoes in half and remove all the seeds with a small spoon or the handle of a spoon.

Place the tomatoes into a bowl with the oil, salt and sugar and mix until the tomatoes are coated. Lay separated on a tray with baking paper on, to avoid getting stuck. Leave to dry in the air for 3-5 hours or until partially dehydrated.

For The Bouillabaisse

Place the oil into a pan and heat up on the stove. Once hot, add the fennel, garlic and red pepper and sweat for 5 minutes. Add the tomato paste and cook out for 1 minute. Add the fish stock, plum tomatoes and saffron. Cook for a further 45 minutes or until reduced by one third. Once reduced, blitz thoroughly and strain. Return to a clean pan and whisk in the butter, double cream and lemon juice. Season to taste.

To Serve

Serve as pictured.

> **Chef's Tip**
>
> Use an over-ripe melon to ensure the flavour breaks through and complements the dish.

PASSION FRUIT MOUSSE, BISCOTTI CRUMB, MANGO, ALMONDS

SERVES 8

🍷 *Valdivieso Eclat Botrytis Semillon, Curico Valley, 2007 (Chile)*

Ingredients

Passion Fruit Mousse

125g passion fruit purée
300ml double cream
150g sugar
1½ leaves gelatine

Biscotti (one large loaf)

60g almonds (toasted, roughly chopped)
510g plain flour
13g Ultratex (similar to xanthan gum)
1½ tsp baking powder
1½ tsp baking soda
1 tsp salt
110g unsalted butter
340g sugar
4 eggs
1 orange (zest of)

Sugared Almonds (15 portions)

150g almonds (*blanched*)
200ml stock syrup (see page 231)
100g caster sugar

Mango Pastille (12 portions)

1 large mango (firm but ripe)
140g mango purée
220g caster sugar

Garnish

quenelle of Cornish clotted cream ice cream (optional)
crème anglais (drizzle of)

16 x hemisphere moulds

Method

For The Passion Fruit Mousse
Heat up the purée in a pan. Soak the gelatine in a little water and add to the purée. Semi-whip the cream and sugar, and slowly add the purée.

Pipe into hemisphere moulds and freeze. When frozen, put 2 hemispheres together to form a sphere.

For The Biscotti
Preheat the oven to 180°C. Cream together the butter and sugar, then add the eggs 1 at a time, followed by the zest. Combine the almonds, baking powder, baking soda, flour, Ultratex and salt, then add to the butter mix. Mix thoroughly (the dough will be sticky). Form the dough into a log, place on a baking tray and put into your hot oven for 20-25 minutes until it begins to brown. Turn the oven down to 160°C and bake for a further 20 minutes.

When completely cool, slice into 1cm slices.

Heat the oven to 140°C (do not use a fan oven) and return the biscotti to the oven. Bake for approximately 10 minutes until crisp and lightly golden. Leave to cool. Pulse in a processor to a big crumb. Store in an airtight container with silica gel.

For The Sugared Almonds
Immerse the almonds in a pan with the stock syrup and gently simmer for 1 hour, but do not allow to boil. Drain and reserve the liquid for future use. Place the almonds in the sugar, cover and mix well. Set aside for 1 hour. Sieve the sugar away, reserving for future use. Place the almonds on a baking tray, lined with baking paper or a silicon sheet. Roast for 9 minutes at 160°C until lightly golden. Remove and allow to cool. Store in an airtight container.

For The Mango Pastille (Prepare 1 week in advance for best results)
Remove the stone and skin from the mango. Slice the flesh into ½cm slices, then cut into 1cm pieces.

Mix the mango purée with 20g of the caster sugar and bring it carefully to a simmer. When warmed through, remove from the heat and add the mango batons. Leave to infuse for 1 hour. Drain carefully, removing as much liquid as possible. Cover the mango pieces with more sugar, carefully separating them. Cover with the rest of the sugar to submerge the mango and leave, preferably for 1 week, to dry.

> **Chef's Tip**
> If you are struggling to get ripe mangoes, you can store them on a bed of dry rice a few days prior to cooking.

To Serve
Carefully roll the passion fruit balls in the biscotti crumb and plate as pictured.

040
THE BATH PRIORY
HOTEL, RESTAURANT & SPA

Weston Road, Bath, BA1 2XT

01225 331 922
www.thebathpriory.co.uk

The Bath Priory Hotel, Restaurant and Spa is a sublime luxury hotel located a short stroll from the Georgian city of Bath. Indulgence and relaxation take on new meaning with the hotel's individually designed rooms, a spectacular Garden Spa and, of course, the renowned and beautifully decorated restaurant that overlooks the expanse of award-winning gardens.

Under the direction of Michelin-starred executive chef Sam Moody, the restaurant serves superb modern European cuisine. Sam has created a reputation for exciting flavours, fine quality food and the delivery of a culinary experience that will delight time and again. Sam has a genuine passion for developing menus that use fresh, local ingredients. His supplier relationships are very strong, his salad leaves are grown locally and to his precise requirements: the link between food and cuisine does not come much closer than this. Of course the most local supplier is the Priory's own kitchen garden. The planting here is a collaboration between kitchen and garden, with some interesting experimentation and some fine produce making its way direct from paddock to plate. Sam's superb cuisine is complemented by an exemplary wine list.

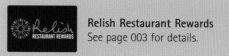

Relish Restaurant Rewards
See page 003 for details.

There is much to love about this divine hotel, which maintains its typical country house hotel character and atmosphere, while boasting an award-winning restaurant that continues to delight under the direction of Michelin-starred executive chef Sam Moody.

FRIED PHEASANT EGG, WHITE WYE VALLEY ASPARAGUS, MUSHROOM DUXELLE, TRUFFLE

SERVES 6

🍷 *Alsace Muscat, Domaine Trimbach, Réserve 2011 (France)*

Ingredients

6 pheasant eggs
200g fresh wild mushrooms (5 per portion)
50g butter

Mushroom Duxelle

500g button mushrooms (thinly sliced)
1 shallot (diced)
25g butter
75ml Madeira
75ml double cream
salt and pepper

Asparagus Spears

12 spears white asparagus
1 lemon (zest and juice of)
olive oil
salt and pepper

Caramelised Shallot Purée

7 shallots
25g butter
chervil oil

To Garnish

picked chervil
fresh truffle (to grate)
chervil oil
lemon (squeeze of)

Method

For The Mushroom Duxelle

Melt the butter in a wide, heavy-bottomed pan and sweat the shallot off for 5 minutes. Add the button mushrooms, season well and cook over a medium to high heat for 10-15 minutes, stirring from time to time. Once cooked down, add the cream, reduce by half, then add the Madeira and reduce by half again. Pulse in a food processor until an even, small texture is achieved.

For The Asparagus Spears

Preheat the oven to 160ºC.

Peel and grade each spear. Lightly season with salt, pepper, and the lemon zest and juice. Coat with olive oil.

Lay out a 45cm sheet of tin foil, topped with a 45cm sheet of silicon, then lay the asparagus out, folding over so it is covered with the silicon and tin foil - creating an airtight cooking pouch.

Bake for 3-5 minutes or until soft. Leave to cool.

To finish, heat a non-stick pan, and char the asparagus for 2 minutes on each side.

For The Caramelised Shallot Purée

Sweat the shallots with the butter and oil until dark golden, but not burnt. Add a little water, then blend and pass through a fine mesh sieve. Adjust seasoning and acidity with lemon juice.

To Finish

Heat a non-stick pan, add 50g butter, allow to foam, then turn off the heat, add the eggs and slow fry them over a very gentle heat for 8-12 minutes. Once the white has set, remove onto kitchen tissue. Increase the heat and fry the wild mushrooms with a pinch of salt and a little squeeze of lemon.

To Serve

Assemble as in the photograph.

WARM ESCABECHE OF LOCAL PARTRIDGE, WITH SMOKED BACON, APPLE, GARDEN VEGETABLES & LIGHT GAME JUS

SERVES 6

 Valtellina Superiore, Nino Negri, Mazer, Inferno 2009 (Italy)

Ingredients

6 partridges (oven ready, lightly seasoned)
50g butter

Vegetables
6 chestnut mushrooms (shaved)
1 carrot, 1 baby leek, 9 turnips, 9 radish, 2 chard stalks (anything with good texture and in season)
2 apples (diced)

Smoked Bacon
200g smoked belly pork (boneless, rindless)
1 leek (halved), 1 onion, 1 carrot, 1 stick celery
1 bulb garlic (halved), 1 tsp coriander seeds
1 tsp black peppercorns, 1 tsp cloves
water (to cover)
1 tbsp flour, oil (for frying)

Game Jus
1kg partridge carcass (chopped)
30ml unscented oil
1 small onion (cut into rings)
2 bulbs garlic (halved widthways, unpeeled)
10 sprigs thyme, 20 sprigs tarragon
1 vanilla pod (scraped), 20 white peppercorns
500ml water, 1 litre chicken stock

Escabeche
250g shallots (finely sliced)
250ml extra virgin olive oil
75ml Xeres, Valdespino or Olorosso vinegar

Garnish
hazelnuts, girolles (panfried)

Chef's Tip
For this recipe you don't need much smoked bacon, but it keeps very well and freezes perfectly so it's worth cooking as big a piece as your pot will allow and saving it for another meal. The stock is good for soups, purées and sauces.

Method

For The Escabeche
Sweat the shallots in the olive oil until lightly caramelised. Add the vinegar and simmer for 1-2 minutes. Adjust seasoning, cool.

For The Smoked Bacon (Prepare the day before)
Place all the ingredients in a pot, bring to a simmer and cook for 2-3 hours or until soft. Remove the pork and press between 2 trays with a heavy weight on top and place in the fridge for 12 hours. Dice into 20mm cubes. Lightly flour and caramelise on all sides.

For The Vegetables
Split the baby leek through the middle and *blanch* for 2 minutes. Shave the carrots on a *mandolin* and *blanch*, 30 seconds. Baton the chard stalks and *blanch*, 30 seconds. Halve the radishes and turnips and then *blanch* for 30 seconds. Mix the diced apple with the *blanched* vegetables. Thinly slice the mushrooms and keep raw.

For The Partridge
Place the partridge into a hot, heavy-bottomed pan, legs down, in a little oil. Over a high heat, start to roast the partridge, then place into the oven and cook for 1 minute. Turn and cook for a further 4 minutes. Now add 50g butter, turn onto the breast and roast for a final 2 minutes. Remove from the pan and place on a tray. Pour over the excess cooking fat and allow to rest for 15 minutes.

Game Jus
Preheat a deep roasting pan in the oven at 180°C. Add the oil and brown the carcass on all sides, then add the onion rings and lightly colour before adding the garlic, tarragon and thyme and vanilla.

Cool the pan down by adding the water first, then the chicken stock and peppercorns. Bring to the boil, then simmer for 1 hour, pass through a colander and then a sieve. Return to a saucepan then reduce, skimming from time to time. Correct seasoning and pass through muslin.

To Finish And Serve
Warm the escabeche to about 50°C.

Remove the thigh and breast meat from the bone and drop the meat into the escabeche. Add the vegetables and mix well. Drain and arrange on a warmed plate, along with the smoked bacon and game *jus*. Garnish with hazelnuts and girolles if desired.

STAR ANISE ROAST PINEAPPLE WITH SMITH APPLES & CHANTILLY

SERVES 6

🍷 *Sauvignon Blanc Noble Late Harvest, Mulderbosch 2009 (South Africa)*

Ingredients

Roast Pineapple

1 pineapple (peeled, cored and quartered)
200g caster sugar
20ml water
5 star anise
1 vanilla pod (halved and seeds scraped)
25g butter

Chantilly

200ml double cream
1 vanilla pod (halved and seeds scraped)
10g icing sugar

1 Granny Smith apple

Method

For The Roast Pineapple

Add the water, sugar, star anise, and vanilla to a pan, stir once then leave to make a caramel. Add the pineapple and cook on a gentle heat for 10 minutes. Remove from the heat, add the butter and cover. Allow to stand until needed.

For The Chantilly

Mix all ingredients together. Whip to peaks.

To Serve

Shave the apple on a *mandolin*. Arrange the pineapple on your plate with a couple of scoops of chantilly, then top with the thinly shaved apple. Dress the plate with a drizzle of the roast pineapple syrup.

050
BEAMINSTER BRASSERIE

The BridgeHouse Hotel, 3 Prout Bridge, Beaminster, Dorset, DT8 3AY

01308 862 200
www.beaminsterbrasserie.co.uk

The 700-year-old BridgeHouse is a listed ancient monument and provides a sophisticated location in which to enjoy contemporary British food. Located in the picturesque Brit Valley, it was originally a home for 12 priests and was bought nine years ago by restaurateurs Mark and Joanna Donovan, who have created an idyllic 40-cover restaurant in the sumptuous Georgian panelled room.

BridgeHouse combines trend and tradition. There are vast inglenook fireplaces, stone mullioned windows and oak beams alongside contemporary artwork and individually painted lampshades by popular London artists.

The two AA rosette restaurant is overseen by the Michelin-trained head chef Steve Pielesz, who has added style and panache to the BridgeHouse restaurant, The Beaminster Brasserie, during his four year tenure. He favours robust, seasonal flavours and presents his dishes with no little flair.

"We are fortunate here in Dorset to be surrounded by a sensational natural larder from land and sea," says Steve. "Exceptional produce is right on our doorstep." Steve even has his own vineyard in the gardens of BridgeHouse which provide a steady supply of fruit.

BridgeHouse, recently winning the Dorset Tourism Gold Award for Hotel of the Year 2013 and Taste of the West 2013 Gold Award, offers high-end accommodation for guests in its 13 three AA starred rooms. The hotel has been refurbished and styled by Mark and Joanna and is just a ten minute drive from the Jurassic Coast. The hotel makes up part of the town immortalised in Hardy's Tess of the D'Urbervilles, in which it was renamed Emminster. More recently, the area was included in a movie version of Far from the Madding Crowd.

Relish Restaurant Rewards
See page 003 for details.

ster
rie

Larders don't get much better than the one on the doorstep of The BridgeHouse. Its location, just six miles from the Jurassic Coast, means its kitchen receives a plentiful supply of daily boat fish, foraged ingredients, exquisite meat and exceptional market garden produce.

Mark and Joanna were formerly regular visitors to BridgeHouse as guests and liked the place so much that they bought it. "We have a great team here at BridgeHouse including Steve Pielesz as executive chef and sous chef Geraldine Gay." says Mark.

"We never rest on our laurels, we continually strive for excellence."

AA

★★★
Hotel

LYME BAY SCALLOPS, CONFIT PORK BELLY, PARSNIP, APPLE & WATERCRESS PUREE, LOBSTER REDUCTION, APPLE GEL

SERVES 6

Bacchus Fumé 2010 - Furleigh Estate, Netherbury, Dorset (England)

Ingredients

Pork Belly Confit
1kg pork belly (skin on)
sea salt (pinch of)
black pepper (pinch of)
1 litre duck fat
5 cloves garlic
1 orange (rind of)
6 star anise
12 black peppercorns
1 chilli (de-seeded)

Scallops
18 fresh scallops (roe on)
1 tsp rapeseed oil, 50g butter
½ lemon (juice of)
salt and pepper (to season)

Purée
4 parsnips (peeled)
2 red devil apples (peeled and cored)
2 bunches watercress
1 litre vegetable stock (or bouillon)
100g butter
salt and pepper

Lobster Reduction
2 lobsters (shells of)
1 stick celery, ½ onion, 1 carrot
2 cloves garlic, ½ leek
50ml brandy
1 tbsp tomato purée
200ml good fish stock
50g butter

Apple Gel
250ml good quality apple juice
2g agar agar

Garnish
micro celery leaves

Method

For The Pork Belly (Prepare 12 hours before)

Rub a good pinch of sea salt and black pepper over the pork belly and leave covered for 12 hours. Preheat the oven to 130ºC and place the belly in a deep dish roasting tray. Cover with the duck fat and the rest of the ingredients, then cover with tin foil and cook for 3½ hours. Allow to cool, then press with a weight until chilled completely. Cut into cubes before serving.

For The Scallops

Season the scallops with sea salt and black pepper. Heat a non-stick frying pan, add some rapeseed oil and place the scallops flat side down. Do not move them until they begin to caramelise. Add the butter and when it foams, add the lemon. Turn just before serving.

For The Purée

Heat the vegetable stock or bouillon. Chop the parsnips and cook until soft. Add the apples and cook until soft, then add the watercress and leave for 30 seconds. Drain well and pat dry between a clean cloth. Place into a blender with the butter and blend until smooth.

For The Lobster Reduction

Chop all the vegetables and heat in a large saucepan. Add the lobster shells and brandy. Stir in the tomato purée and stock, then cook for 30 minutes. Liquidise and pass through a sieve. Reduce by half then stir in the butter.

For The Apple Gel

Place the apple juice in a pan and warm through. Add the agar agar, simmer for 10 minutes or until the agar has dissolved. Leave to cool. Once the jelly has set, transfer to a food processor and blitz until smooth. Place in a piping bag and refrigerate.

To Serve

Heat the parsnip purée and arrange the seared scallops on top, with 2 cubes of the pork belly in-between. Spoon the lobster reduction around. Add the apple gel and micro celery leaves.

LINE CAUGHT SEA BASS, CRAB BONBONS, FENNEL & PAK CHOI TIGERS, TERIYAKI SAUCE

SERVES 6

Meursault Les Tillets 2009, Bourgogne (France)

Ingredients

9 tiger prawns
6 x 120g fillet sea bass
butter (knob of)

Crab Bonbons

150g white crabmeat
150g brown crabmeat
50g fresh coriander (chopped)
1 tbsp sweet chilli sauce
½ lemon (juice of)
salt and pepper (pinch of)
plain flour, egg (beaten) and Panko breadcrumbs
(to *pané*)

Fennel And Pak Choi

2 heads fennel
3 pak choi
1 small pack egg noodles
1 tbsp sesame oil
1 tsp rice vinegar
sesame seeds (sprinkle of)

Teriyaki Sauce

3 cloves garlic (finely sliced)
1 finger fresh ginger (cut into thin strips)
50ml soy sauce
300ml mirin
150ml sake
2 tsp cornflour
1 tsp arrowroot
1 tbsp water
50g Demerara sugar
sesame seeds (sprinkle of)

Method

For The Sea Bass

Heat a flat-based frying pan. Place the fish in the pan, skin-side down, and cook on a medium heat for about 2 minutes. Add a knob of butter then turn just before serving.

For The Crab Bonbons

Mix the crab, coriander, sweet chilli sauce, lemon juice and seasoning together, then mould into 18 equal sized balls. Roll in flour, then egg wash and then Panko breadcrumbs. Refrigerate before deep frying.

For The Fennel And Pak Choi

Thinly slice the fennel and pak choi. *Blanch* the egg noodles. Lightly sauté the fennel in the sesame oil. Add the pak choi and noodles to heat through. Finish with the rice vinegar and sprinkle with sesame seeds.

For The Teriyaki Sauce

Add the garlic and ginger to the soy, mirin and sake in a pan. Bring to the boil. Dilute the cornflour and arrowroot in the tablespoon of water, then use to lightly thicken the sauce. Add a little at a time so as not to make it too thick. Add the sugar to taste and sprinkle with sesame seeds.

For The Tigers

Shell the tiger prawns and halve lengthways. Just before serving, add the prawns into the hot teriyaki sauce for about 30 seconds to heat through.

To Serve

Arrange some stir fry into the middle of the plate and place the sea bass on top. Deep fry the bonbons until golden. Arrange the 3 bonbons around the dish with the 3 halves of tiger prawns. Spoon over the teriyaki sauce.

WARM PISTACHIO CAKE, POACHED PEAR, GINGER BEER GEL, BLACKBERRY ICE CREAM

SERVES 6

 Monbazillac Chateau Septy 2009 (France)

Ingredients

Pistachio Cake

180g butter
375g sugar
6 eggs
75g plain flour
2 tsp baking powder
1 lemon (zest of)
300g ground pistachios
300g ground almonds
honey (to drizzle, see tip)

Blackberry Ice Cream

150g fresh blackberries
225g sugar
4 egg yolks
560ml double cream

Ginger Beer Gel

250ml ginger beer
2g agar agar

Pear Purée

2 fresh pears (peeled, cored and
roughly chopped)
25g sugar

Pear Crisps

1 fresh pear (thinly sliced)
200ml water
150g sugar
1 lemon (juice of)

20 x 20cm cake tin (greased and lined)

Method

For The Pistachio Cake

Preheat the oven to 180°C. Whisk together the butter and sugar until pale and fluffy. Add the eggs with a little of the flour, mixing well. Add the lemon zest and baking powder. Gently fold in the rest of the flour, pistachios and almonds. Pour into the prepared tin and bake for 20-25 minutes or until a skewer comes out clean.

> **Chef's Tip**
>
> Once out of the oven, prick the cake and drizzle with warm honey and additional pistachios.

For The Blackberry Ice Cream

Gently cook the blackberries in a pan with 30g of the sugar until some juice begins to seep out. Leave to cool. Warm the cream in a pan but do not allow it to boil. Whisk together the egg yolks and remaining sugar until pale, then whisk in the warmed cream and cooled blackberries. Place the mix into an ice cream machine and churn, or see page 231 if you don't have an ice cream maker. Transfer to the freezer.

For The Ginger Beer Gel

Warm the ginger beer in a pan. Add the agar agar then simmer for 10 minutes, or until the agar has dissolved. Leave to cool. Once the jelly has set, blitz in a food processor then transfer to a piping bag and refrigerate.

For The Pear Purée

Place the pears in a pan with the sugar and a little water, then cook until soft. Once cooked, place in a food processor and blitz to a purée.

For The Pear Crisps

Place the water and sugar in a pan. Boil for 10 minutes to produce a syrup then leave to cool. Thinly slice the pear (using a *mandolin* helps). Sprinkle the lemon juice over the sliced pear to stop it from going brown. Pour the syrup over the pear slices to coat them, removing any excess liquid. Arrange them on a lined tray and leave to dry out in an oven set to 50°C overnight or use a dehydrator.

To Serve

Plate as pictured.

060
BLAGDON MANOR
RESTAURANT WITH ROOMS

Ashwater, Devon, EX21 5DF

01409 211 224
www.blagdon.com

O n a sunny day, the views of the undulating Devonshire hills, which stretch for more than 35 miles from Blagdon Manor's sumptuous dining room, are breathtaking.

But that's not the most impressive aspect of the restaurant. Chef Steve Morey conjures dreamlike dishes that combine the best of local and seasonal flavours. Steve and his wife, Liz, have owned Blagdon for 12 years, where they operate a must-visit destination on the south west's fine dining scene.

Tucked away in rolling countryside, the restaurant with rooms has an impressive heritage. A dwelling on the site was listed in the Domesday Book, and the current buildings date back to the 17th Century.

These buildings have been tastefully refined and extended by Steve and Liz during their tenure, and their immaculately manicured gardens extend to more than three acres and are filled with herbaceous borders, seasonal flowers, a bowling-green-esque lawn and plenty of other impressive horticultural features.

Inside, Blagdon has everything to make guests feel comfortable. Two dining rooms, a library, a sophisticated bar and a lounge give people plenty of space in which to relax. The dining rooms look over Yes Tor, on Dartmoor, and there are six tastefully decorated en-suite rooms, each with a garden view.

Steve's pedigree is impressive indeed. With a background at La Gavroche, he has worked with some of the UK's best and most influential chefs and hoteliers of the past 30 years. He worked briefly under Albert Roux and then with Michel Roux Jr.

When asked what style of cooking he produces, his answer would be: "I just cook using the best of local produce when it is in season."

Relish Restaurant Rewards
See page 003 for details.

Five star accommodation with luxury fittings
provides a haven for travellers who want to relax in
exquisite surrounds. Guests can enjoy Devonshire's
stunning countryside in a peaceful, tranquil location
before decamping to the restaurant for breakfast.

Steve and Liz provide a personal, bespoke service at Blagdon Manor for guests who expect nothing but the best. Their rooms are dog-friendly, and travellers are likely to meet their own chocolate Labradors, Mace and Cassia - better known as the 'Blagdon Spice Girls.'

WARM SMOKED SALMON, PICKLED CUCUMBER, YOGHURT & CAVIAR

SERVES 4

🍷 *Knightor Winery Madeleine Angevine, Trethurgy (Cornwall)*

Ingredients

4 x 100g pieces Cornish smoked salmon
4 new potatoes
1 cucumber (flesh of)
1 tsp sea salt
1 tsp white wine vinegar
100g yoghurt
4 tsp caviar

Cucumber Sauce

100ml white wine
100ml fish stock
200ml double cream
1 cucumber (skin of)

Garnish

mustard
watercress (freshly chopped)
tomato (diced)
chives (chopped)

Method

For The Potatoes

Cook the new potatoes in simmering salted water until they are cooked through but still slightly firm, then leave to cool in the water.

For The Cucumber

Peel the cucumber, keeping the skin aside to make the cucumber fish sauce.

Halve the cucumber lengthways and remove the seeds with a teaspoon. Slice the cucumber halves thinly, lengthways, then place into a bowl with a little sea salt. Leave to one side - the salt will draw out the water. After about 15 minutes, tip off the water then add a teaspoon of sugar and white wine vinegar.

For The Sauce

Reduce the white wine by half, add the fish stock, then reduce again by half. Add the cream and bring to the boil. Combine the sauce with the reserved cucumber skin, liquidise and pass through a fine sieve.

To Serve

Put the salmon into a warm pan on the side of the stove, just to warm it through. Cut each potato into 3 slices and chargrill, then put them into the pan with salmon to keep warm. Assemble the dish as pictured finishing with yoghurt, tomato dice, mustard and cress, the cucumber fish sauce and caviar.

> **Chef's Tip**
>
> Before you put the cucumber sauce on the plate, blitz it with a hand blender. This puts lots of air into the sauce and makes it nice and light.

BREAST OF PHEASANT, BEER BATTERED CORNED BEEF, TRUFFLED CABBAGE, ALMOND CROQUETTE POTATOES & BEETROOT

SERVES 4

🍷 *Costières de Nîmes, Château Sainte Elisabeth (France)*

Ingredients

4 breasts local pheasant

Croquettes

500g potatoes
75g butter
plain flour (to coat)
2-3 eggs (for eggwash)
100g ground almonds
100g breadcrumbs
salt and pepper (to season)

Beetroot Sauce

500g beetroot (peeled, keep some aside to garnish)
1 litre beef stock

Truffled Cabbage

300g Savoy cabbage
1 tsp truffle peelings

Corned Beef Fritters

200g corned beef
100g tempura flour
small bottle light beer

Garnish

seasonal vegetables and beetroot (panfried)

Method

For The Croquettes

Cook the potatoes in boiling salted water. Drain when cooked, then dry. Mash and mix in the butter. When cool enough, roll into walnut sized balls. Combine the breadcrumbs with the ground almonds, and season the flour. Coat the potato balls first with the seasoned flour, then with eggwash and finally with the ground almonds and breadcrumbs. Fry the croquettes at the same time as the fritters.

For The Beetroot Sauce

Cook the beetroot in boiling salted water until tender, then leave to cool in the water. Reduce the beef stock by half. Strain the cooled beetroot and liquidise with the beef stock. Pass through a fine sieve.

For The Cabbage

Pick the leaves off the stalks and tear into small pieces, then cook in boiling salted water. When cooked, place into iced cold water to refresh. Warm the cabbage in a little butter with some truffle peelings just as you are about to serve.

For The Corned Beef Fritters

Dice the corned beef into bite-size chunks. Mix the tempura flour very lightly with the beer, then toss the corned beef into the batter and deep fry at 180ºC just before serving.

> **Chef's Tip**
>
> If you can't get tempura flour, you can use self-raising flour for the fritter batter.

For The Pheasant

Preheat the oven to 180ºC. Seal the 4 breasts on all sides and cook in the oven for 5-6 minutes, then leave to rest. Halve each breast just before serving, as pictured.

To Serve

Assemble dish as shown in picture.

ICED MINT PARFAIT

SERVES 4

 Campbells Rutherglen Muscat (Australia)

Ingredients

Parfait

4 eggs
10 egg yolks
250g caster sugar
1 litre double cream (whipped)
1 box After Eight mints
20ml Crème de Menthe

Gratin

5 egg yolks
125g sugar
50ml Crème de Cassis
125ml double cream (whipped)

Mini Doughnuts

8 slices white bread
lemon curd
100g tempura flour
small bottle ginger beer
2 egg whites
oil (to deep fry)
100g caster sugar

Popcorn

100g honey
100g butter
100g sugar
1 tsp bicarbonate of soda
100g popcorn kernels

Garnish

100g white chocolate (melted)
red berry coulis
strawberries (quartered)
raspberries
Thai basil leaves

4 x 100g *dariole* moulds

Method

For The Parfait

Put the After Eight mints into the freezer and leave until hard. Once frozen, grind these using a food processor, until you have a fine powder.

Whisk the eggs, egg yolks and caster sugar into a *sabayon* over a water bath, or *bain-marie*, until the ribbon stage is achieved. Once thick, remove and keep whisking until cold. Gently fold in the whipped double cream, slowly add the Crème de Menthe and finally fold in the After Eight powder. Gently pour into stainless steel *dariole* moulds and freeze.

> **Chef's Tip**
>
> I have tried making the parfait in smaller quantities but it just seems lighter when making this amount. This mix makes about 24 *dariole* moulds worth so use the 4 that you need and keep the rest for next time!

For The Gratin Mix

Whisk the egg yolks, sugar and Crème de Cassis into a *sabayon* over a water bath until the ribbon stage is achieved. Take off the heat and whisk until cold, then fold in the whipped double cream. Keep in the fridge.

For The Toffee Popcorn

Make some plain popcorn with a popcorn machine or on the hob. You may also use ready-made plain popcorn.

Place the honey, butter and sugar into a pan over a low heat. When the sugar has dissolved, turn up the heat and cook until it reaches 127°C (hard ball stage). Take off the heat, add the bicarbonate of soda and stir in the popcorn. Spread the popcorn on baking sheets and dry out in the oven at 125°C for 30 minutes, turning every 10 minutes. When cool, dip in melted white chocolate.

For The Mini Doughnuts

Cut out the slices of bread into 9 small discs per person, making 36 discs in total. 12 of the discs need to have a smaller hole cut out in the middle to make a ring. Place a ring on top of a disc and put a teaspoon of lemon curd into the recess, then place another disc on the top. Repeat with the other rings and discs, so you end up with 12. Lightly coat the doughnuts in egg white. Mix the tempura flour with the ginger beer, coat the doughnuts and deep fry for about 5 minutes at 180°C until golden. Remove from the oil onto kitchen paper and then roll in caster sugar.

To Serve

Arrange the raspberries on your plate, spoon over a little of the gratin mix and use a blow torch to turn the mix golden. Assemble as pictured.

070
GIDLEIGH PARK

Chagford, Devon, TQ13 8HH

01647 432 367
www.gidleigh.com

This quintessential country house is nestled in a wooded valley within the natural beauty of the wilds of Dartmoor, Devon. Home to the much loved two Michelin-starred executive chef Michael Caines MBE, its location is breathtaking and the views are something else altogether. Taking in the gardens and grounds of the estate and the river running through, the house is a spectacular backdrop to showcase an eclectic art and antique collection. The journey to Gidleigh is often made by those seeking to enjoy one of the finest dining experiences in the UK.

Michael Caines continues to develop his cuisine, using the very finest local produce and his exceptional culinary skills to great appreciation. As one would expect, the dining experience is matched with one of the finest cellars in the UK, holding over 1,300 bins under the expert guidance of master sommelier, Edouard Oger. Adding to the five star experience, the bedrooms at Gidleigh Park are of exceptional luxury. All individual in style and design, they feature the most stunning bathrooms, wet rooms and spa suites that inspire a true sense of indulgence.

Relish Restaurant Rewards
See page 003 for details.

A visit to the Restaurant at Gidleigh Park
is an experience completed by the imposing
backdrop of the surrounding countryside,
the stylish interior, genuine warmth of the
team, fine wine and two Michelin-starred
food created by Michael Caines MBE

WARM LOBSTER SALAD WITH MANGO, LIME & CARDAMOM VINAIGRETTE & CURRIED MAYONNAISE

SERVES 4

 Gut Oggau, Grüner Veltliner & Welschriesling, Theodora 2012 (Austria)

Ingredients

Lobster
2 x 500g lobsters (cooked in *court-bouillon*)
4 lobster claws, olive oil or lobster oil (if available)
¼ tsp ground cardamom

Curried Mayonnaise
10g Madras curry powder
15ml vegetable oil, 150g mayonnaise
150g Greek yoghurt
lime (juice of), salt

Cardamom Gastric
20g cardamom pods
200g stock syrup (see page 231), 45g glucose
60ml lime juice, ½ lime (fine zest)

Mango, Lime And Cardamom Vinaigrette
175g frozen Alfonso mango purée
cardamom gastric (see above, reserve some of
the gastric to serve)
50ml groundnut oil or good quality vegetable oil
salt and freshly ground black pepper
lime juice (to taste)

Potato, Mango And Lobster Salad
75g Ratte potatoes, or firm waxy salad potatoes
(cooked, diced)
75g ripe mango (diced)
75g lobster meat (diced)
¼ tsp fresh basil (finely chopped)
¼ lime (zest of, finely grated)
30g curried mayonnaise (see above)
lime juice (squeeze of)

Garnish
fresh micro salad: basil (green and purple),
coriander and lemon balm
fresh chive flowers (if available)
lime (zest of), ground cardamom (for dusting)
caviar (optional)

Method

For The Lobster
Cut the lobster tails in half, then cut each half into 4 pieces. Reserve on a baking tray for later. Cut the claws in half across the middle so they can stand up. Dice the rest of the tail meat for the salad.

For The Curried Mayonnaise
Toast the curry powder in a dry pan, add the vegetable oil and leave to infuse. Mix together the mayonnaise and yoghurt in a bowl, then pour in the curried oil through a sieve and whisk. Add lime juice and salt to taste. Set aside in the fridge.

> **Chef's Tip**
> I put my mayonnaise in a squeezy bottle and pipe it. It gives a cleaner, neater finish to a dish when it is used as a garnish.

For The Cardamom Gastric
Blend the cardamom pods in a food processor until broken up. Roast the cardamom seeds in a dry pan until they release their aroma, then add the stock syrup. Bring to the boil, and cook until it reaches 110°C and has reduced. Add the glucose, lime juice and zest. Bring back to the boil and heat to 110°C. Strain the gastric through a sieve, pressing well with a ladle. Set aside.

For The Mango And Lime Vinaigrette
Blend the mango purée and the cardamom gastric. Add the groundnut oil, season with salt and pepper, and add a little lime juice if needed. Leave to cool.

For The Potato, Mango And Salad
Mix the potato, mango and lobster with the chopped basil, lime zest and the curried mayonnaise in a bowl. Season with salt and pepper and a squeeze of lime juice.

To Assemble
Preheat the oven to 170°C. Brush the lobster with olive or lobster oil, dust with the cardamom and transfer to the oven for 5 minutes. Pour some mango, lime and cardamom vinaigrette onto each plate and drizzle over some of the reserved cardamom gastric. *Quenelle* the lobster salad mixture and place in the middle of each plate. Remove the lobster pieces from the oven and squeeze some lime juice over them. Place 1 claw and 4 pieces of tail on each plate and spoon any oil from the pan over and around. Pipe 5 dots of curried mayonnaise on each plate then finish with the herbs, grated lime zest and a dusting of freshly ground cardamom.

BOCADDON FARM ROSE VEAL, SHERRY CREAM SAUCE & TOMATO FONDUE

SERVES 4

 Cerasuolo di Vittoria, Cos 2010
(Italy)

Ingredients

Veal
4 x 180g rosé veal fillet pieces (seasoned with
salt and pepper)
1 large clove garlic, 1 sprig fresh thyme
50g butter, 2 tbsp vegetable oil

Mushrooms
160g morels or wild mushrooms
(eg: mousserons, girolles, pieds bleu)
10g butter

Tomato Fondue
8 whole plum tomatoes
40ml olive oil, 40g onions (chopped)
1½ cloves garlic (finely chopped)
3g fresh thyme (finely chopped)
salt and freshly ground black pepper

Baby Gem Lettuce
2 baby gem lettuces (peel the outer leaves)
1 tbsp olive oil, 20g butter
½ clove garlic, 1 small bouquet garni
100ml chicken stock, 20g veal glace (optional)
130ml water
30g smoked bacon trimmings, salt

Watercress Purée
120g watercress, 80g spinach (both wilted)
2 small shallots (sliced, cooked in 15g butter)
8g garlic purée, 75g cream
salt and freshly ground black pepper

Sherry Cream Sauce
100g butter, 40g shallots (sliced)
5 sprigs fresh thyme
50g button mushrooms (sliced, cooked in butter)
100ml dry sherry, 100ml chicken stock
100ml double or whipping cream
100g broad beans (fresh or frozen), asparagus

Chef's Tip
Make the tomato fondue, sherry sauce, watercress
purée and braise the little gems in advance. Reheat
when needed.

Method

For The Tomato Fondue (Preheat the oven to 160°C)
Blanch the tomatoes for 10 seconds in boiling water, refresh in iced water and peel. Cut the top off each tomato one third of the way down, and scoop out the seeds. Reserve the tops for stuffing with fondue later.

Cut the remaining two thirds of each tomato in half and squeeze out the seeds. Heat the olive oil in a heavy-bottomed pan, add the onions and garlic, then cook gently until soft. Add the thyme and tomatoes. Season then stir. Place in the oven for 10 minutes, then stir again. Repeat this process until the tomatoes are dry. Leave to cool.

Stuff the reserved tomato tops with the cooled fondue, place onto a baking tray, brush with olive oil and season. Place in the oven for 10 minutes, then remove and set aside to cool. Wrap and shape into balls in clingfilm and reserve in the fridge for later use. When needed, remove from the clingfilm and reheat in the oven at 160°C.

For The Baby Gem Lettuces
Melt the butter in an ovenproof pan, add the onion and garlic clove and cook gently, without colouring, until the onion is soft. Add the bouquet garni and the rest of the ingredients, apart from the lettuces, and bring to the boil. Add the lettuces, then cover with foil and braise in the oven for 20-30 minutes.

Transfer the lettuces to a rack. Sieve the stock and cool. Warm the lettuce in butter to caramelise just before serving.

For The Watercress Purée
Blend all the ingredients except the cream. Boil the cream, then add it to the mixture and blend again. Season.

For The Sherry Cream Sauce
Melt 50g of butter in a saucepan, and gently cook the shallots and thyme. Add the mushrooms and cook for 3 minutes. Add the sherry and simmer until reduced by half, then add the chicken stock and reduce by half again. Add the cream and reduce by half, then whisk the remaining 50g of butter into the sauce. Pass through a fine sieve, then add the cooked broad beans and button mushrooms to the sauce.

For The Veal
Heat the oil and butter in a pan, add the veal and fry, along with the garlic and sprig of thyme until golden brown. Turn the meat continuously until cooked to preference, then rest. Remove the garlic and skim off the excess fat. *Deglaze* the pan with water and add to your sherry sauce. Bring the sauce to the boil and whisk well, then pass through a fine sieve and keep warm.

To Serve
Drain the mushrooms and broad beans from the warm sauce. Plate as pictured.

RASPBERRY MOUSSE WITH PISTACHIO CREAM & RASPBERRY SORBET

SERVES 4

Maury 2011 Mas Amiel
(France)

Ingredients

Raspberry Mousse
200g raspberries (puréed and sieved)
200g caster sugar, 75ml water
4 egg whites
3 gelatine leaves (soaked, then squeezed)
200ml whipping cream (whipped until thick)

Raspberry Jelly
200g raspberries
40g sugar
½ lemon (juice of), 100ml water
2 gelatine leaves (soaked, then squeezed)

Pistachio Cream
100g crème pâtissière (room temperature),
40g pistachio paste, 4g Kirsch
(whisk together and reserve in a piping bag)

Raspberry Sorbet
500g frozen raspberries
200ml stock syrup (see page 231)
1 lemon (juice of)

Raspberry Ganache
500g raspberry purée (reduced to 300g)
45g trimoline
350g white chocolate, 82g butter

Raspberry Macaroons
300g almonds, 300g icing sugar (sifted together)
5 egg whites (whipped)
250g sugar, 75ml water (heated to 110ºC)
red food colouring

Meringues
200g sugar, 75g water (heated to 110ºC)
6 egg whites (whipped until they start to peak)
2 vanilla pods (seeds scraped)

To Serve
120g raspberries
pistachio nuts (toasted, chopped)

4 x 6cm rings, 4 shot glasses

Method

For The Raspberry Mousse
Dissolve the sugar in 75ml water, then boil to the soft ball stage (120°C). Whisk the egg whites until they form soft peaks. Slowly pour the sugar syrup onto the whites and continue whisking until cold.

Warm some of the purée. Add the gelatine and stir until it melts. Add to the rest of the purée. Cool in the fridge and when it begins to set, fold in the meringue, then the whipped cream. Pipe the mousse into 4 x 6cm rings on a tray lined with baking parchment. Set in fridge.

For The Raspberry Jelly
Heat the raspberries, sugar and lemon juice in a saucepan with 100ml water. Cover and bring to the boil. Remove then drain in a sieve lined with a muslin cloth set over a bowl for about 2 hours so the clear juice filters through. Reserve the cooked raspberries.

Warm a little of the juice, add the gelatine and stir to melt completely. Arrange the cooked raspberries in the bottom of four shot glasses. Fill up the glasses with the juice mixture and leave to set in the fridge.

For The Raspberry Sorbet
Place the frozen raspberries into a deep-sided pan along with the stock syrup and lemon juice. Bring to the boil and cook for 20 minutes. Place into a blender until smooth, then pass through a fine sieve to remove the seeds. Chill in a bowl over ice. Churn in an ice cream machine or see page 231.

For The Raspberry Ganache
Melt the chocolate and butter together. Add the trimoline to the warm, reduced raspberry purée, then combine all the ingredients. Leave to cool, then place into a piping bag.

For The Raspberry Macaroons
Pour the heated sugar and water mix into the whipped egg white and whip until cool. Gently fold the sifted icing sugar and ground almonds into the egg whites until smooth. Pipe immediately and leave to stand for 30 minutes before cooking. Bake at 170ºC for 12-15 minutes until firm, with the oven door ajar. Leave to cool, then sandwich the macaroons with the ganache.

Meringues
Preheat the oven to 100ºC. Slowly pour the cooked sugar onto the whipped egg whites. Add the vanilla seeds and continue whisking until cold. Pipe onto a tray lined with parchment paper. Bake for 1½ hours or until the meringues are crisp and sound hollow when tapped on the base.

To Serve
Assemble as desired. Serve and enjoy!

080
THE HAMBROUGH

Hambrough Road, Ventnor, Isle Of Wight, PO38 1SQ

01983 856 333
www.thehambrough.com

Sitting high above the fishing harbour in Ventnor, The Hambrough restaurant with rooms offers fine dining and boutique accommodation by the sea, on the southern tip of the Isle of Wight. All but one of the seven spacious bedrooms in the Victorian building have magnificent sea views over Ventnor Bay, and have been awarded with five AA stars several years in a row.

Head chef Darren Beevers and sous chef Daniel Perjesi create modern, locally inspired dishes in the 35 cover restaurant. The size of the restaurant allows the chefs to use a majority of local produce. The daily catch comes from only three minutes walk away, eggs come from the nearby farm, meat from six of the island's farms and the vegetables are grown for the restaurant's own specifications.

Darren, originally from Hampshire, works on a principle of three colours and three flavours in his dishes. In his opinion any more will confuse the palate and muddle the dish. His vast Michelin experience has given him a great platform to create unique and visually attractive dishes, showcasing the best of the Isle of Wight's produce.

Relish Restaurant Rewards
See page 003 for details.

Three colours and three flavours are head chef Darren Beevers' motto. "Any more than that confuses the palate and muddles the dish, in my opinion," he says. The Hambrough is lucky enough to be able to source nearly all ingredients from the Isle of Wight, which is 'a luxury,' says Darren.

SMOKED POLLACK, SAUTEED MUSSELS, WILD RICE, KORMA SPICES & CRISPY KALE

SERVES 2

Côtes de Provence Domaine Aureillan Blanc 2012
(France)

Ingredients

Pollack
200g smoked pollack
1 can coconut milk

Curry Purée (a large quantity)
1kg onions (thinly sliced)
75ml Oil of Wight rapeseed oil
15g curry powder
20ml sherry vinegar
100ml double cream

Wild Rice
1 shallot (finely diced)
25ml Oil of Wight rapeseed oil
100g wild rice
50ml white wine

Shallot Bhajis
1 shallot
1 pack tempura flour
5g curry powder
plain flour (to coat)

8 mussels
1 lemon (juice of)
100g kale
oil (for sautéing)
salt and pepper

Chef's Tip

To prevent your onions getting too hot or colouring, add a splash of water to your pan.

Method

For The Curry Purée
Place the onions in a pan on a low heat with 75ml Oil of Wight, season and cook slowly for an hour, without colouring. Add the curry powder, cook for 2 minutes, add the sherry vinegar and reduce, then add the cream. Bring to a simmer and cook out for 5 minutes. Blend and pass through a sieve. Place in a squeezy bottle and reserve.

For The Wild Rice
Cook the shallot gently in the rapeseed oil for 10 minutes. Add the rice and the white wine, reduce, then cover with water and simmer for an hour. Once cooked, season and chill until needed.

For The Shallot Ring Bhajis And Crispy Kale
Mix the tempura flour with water as directed on the packet. Slice the shallot and separate into individual rings. Mix the rings with the curry powder and a splash of lemon juice. Coat in plain flour and then mix with the tempura. Deep fry at 160°C until crisp, then drain on kitchen paper and season. Prepare the kale by removing the frilled leaves from the stalks. Fry the leaves at 160°C until crisp, drain and season.

For The Pollack
Cut the pollack into two 100g pieces. Warm the coconut milk up to 60°C in a pan and place the pollack inside. Poach for 10 minutes. Season the coconut milk after cooking the fish and set aside to froth before serving.

For The Mussels
Wash and rinse the mussels in cold water for 30 minutes. Remove the beard and place in a very hot pan with 100ml of water. Cover with a lid and steam for 1 minute.

Remove the shells and the lips and place the mussels in a hot pan with oil. Sauté each side for approximately 10 seconds.

To Serve
Warm the rice with a touch of seasoning and lemon juice, scatter on the plate, then make artistic dots with the curry purée. Place the pollack pieces on the plate, then the kale, mussels and shallot rings. Using a hand blender or milk foamer, froth up the seasoned coconut milk and spoon on and around the plate.

ROASTED GROUSE WITH BUTTERNUT, CHOCOLATE & LAVENDER

SERVES 2

 Urban Uco Malbec, Mendoza, 2012
(Argentina)

Ingredients

1 large grouse
(ask your butcher to prepare the grouse and
leave on the crown, keeping all the trimmings
for your sauce)
100g salsify (washed, roughly peeled with some
skin left on)
100g chard leaves, 100g green cauliflower

Pastrami Salt

10g juniper berries
10g coriander seeds
10g black pepper, 300g sea salt

Grouse Sauce

1 shallot
grouse bones and trimmings
100ml red wine, 300ml chicken stock
3 fresh lavender heads

Squash Purée

1 butternut squash
(peeled, quartered and de-seeded)
100g butter

Chocolate Sauce

50ml grouse sauce, 10g redcurrant jelly
20g dark chocolate (at least 70% cocoa)

Crumble

50g Panko breadcrumbs
20g pine nuts, 15g duck fat

Grouse Sausage

meat from the grouse legs, 100g chicken breast
1 egg, 150ml double cream
1 tsp flat-leaf parsley (chopped)

Chef's Tip

Most chefs recommend that you soak the salsify
in lemon water to prevent it from discolouring, but
not doing so gives it a different look.

Method

For The Pastrami Salt (Prepare 2 hours in advance)
Toast the berries, seeds and pepper then blend with the salt.
Use to thoroughly season the grouse and leave for 2 hours.

For The Grouse Sauce
Roast the shallot, grouse bones and trimmings for 30 minutes
at 180°C. Place into a pan with the red wine and reduce by half,
then add the stock. Simmer for 2 hours, then pass through a
sieve, pressing down on the trimmings. Reduce to approximately
100ml, remove from the heat. Add the lavender, cover and leave
to infuse.

For The Squash Purée
Chop the top quarter into small squares and set aside. Dice the
remainder. Melt the butter in a pan, then add the diced squash.
Season and sweat until tender, for about 45 minutes.
Add a splash of water, blend and pass through a sieve. Keep in a
squeezy bottle for later.

For The Chocolate Sauce
Warm the 500ml of grouse sauce with the redcurrant jelly, then
take it off the heat and whisk in the dark chocolate. Season.

For The Crumble
Melt the duck fat in a pan, add the Panko breadcrumbs and pine
nuts, then gently cook until coloured.

For The Grouse And Vegetables
Cut the salsify into batons and boil in salted water for 10
minutes, or until tender. Set aside.

Prepare the cauliflower into small florets, place into boiling
salted water along with the reserved squash for 1 minute,
then remove.

Preheat the oven to 180°C. Sear the grouse in a hot pan, baste
with 15g of butter and place in the oven. Roast for 10 minutes,
cover in foil and rest for 10 minutes. Whilst the grouse is resting,
heat all the vegetables in a frying pan with a touch of butter,
adding the chard leaves right at the end as they only need 10
seconds of heat. Season.

For The Grouse Sausage
Take the meat off the grouse legs and blend with 100g chicken
breast. Add 1 egg and blend in the double cream. Pass through
a sieve then mix in the chopped parsley. Roll in clingfilm to
create a sausage shape. Steam at 95°C for 12 minutes.

To Serve
Place some dots of squash purée on the plate, arrange the diced
squash, cauliflower and salsify. Remove the grouse breasts from
the crown and carve in half lengthways. Top one half of each
breast with the crumble. Spoon the chocolate and grouse sauces
around the plate, then add the grouse breasts, grouse sausage
and the wilted chard leaves.

BLUE CHEESE & WHITE CHOCOLATE GANACHE WITH WALNUT FRANGIPANE, WALNUT MOUSSELINE & CELERY SORBET

SERVES 12

Domaine de l'Ancienne Cure Monbazillac 2010 (France)

Ingredients

Ganache
120g Isle of Wight soft blue cheese
120ml double cream
120g Philadelphia cheese
400g white chocolate

Frangipane
250g butter (softened)
250g icing sugar
4 eggs (cold)
50g soft plain flour
250g ground walnuts

Mousseline
100g walnuts
200ml milk
200ml double cream

Sorbet
300g celery (roughly chopped)
180ml water
180g sugar
50ml glucose syrup

Tuile
125g caster sugar
100ml glucose syrup
12g butter
100g walnuts

Garnish
Isle of Wight soft blue cheese
celery cress

70mm ring mould

Method

For The Ganache (Prepare the day before)
Break the blue cheese into small pieces. Heat the cream, blue cheese and Philadelphia in a pan, and bring to a gentle boil. Remove from the heat, add the chocolate and blend with a hand blender. Leave overnight to set. Using an electric hand whisk, whisk until pale and light. Chill.

For The Frangipane
Beat the butter and sugar in a machine with a paddle until pale and light. Gradually add the eggs and fold in the flour and ground walnuts. If you can't get ground nuts, you can blitz them to a powder first in a food processor. Shape using a 70mm ring mould.

For The Mousseline
Simmer the walnuts in the milk on a low heat for an hour or until the nuts are soft and dark brown. Blend together in a blender and then push through a sieve. When cool, softly whip the cream and fold it through the walnut purée. Chill.

For The Sorbet
Boil the water, sugar and glucose syrup. Clean the celery. Put all the ingredients in the blender and blitz to a purée. Pass through a sieve, then churn in an ice cream machine.

Chef's Tip
If you don't have an ice cream machine, take a large glass or metal bowl and make sure it fits in your freezer. Pour an inch of water in the bottom and freeze overnight. Take a smaller bowl and place it inside the other, on top of the ice (preferably one which allows 2.5cms between the 2 bowls). Place a tin can or something heavy in the smaller bowl (this should be something that is okay to go in the freezer). Pour water in between the two bowls until it reaches the top. Freeze overnight. Place your sorbet mix into the 'ice bowl' and leave to set overnight. See page 231 for further explanation.

For The Tuile
Mix the sugar, glucose syrup and a splash of water in a pan over a medium heat. Cook until it starts to turn yellow (blond caramel). Add the butter and take off the heat. Mix well and stir in the walnuts. Leave to set. When fully set, smash it up with a rolling pin and blend to a powder in a food processor. Sprinkle evenly on a greaseproof lined baking tray. Bake at 180ºC for approximately 4 minutes until melted. Place another sheet of paper on top and use a rolling pin to spread it evenly over the tray. Leave to set again, and break as required.

To Serve
Serve as shown in picture.

090
HARBAR BRASSERIE
AT HARBOUR HEIGHTS HOTEL

73 Haven Road, Sandbanks, Poole, Dorset, BH13 7LW

01202 707 272
www.harbourheights.com

Perched on a unique vantage point, with breathtaking panoramic outlooks across the exclusive and world famous Sandbanks Peninsula, Poole Harbour and the beautiful Brownsea Island, Harbour Heights boasts some of the most spectacular views in Dorset.

The Harbar Brasserie is the heart and soul of Harbour Heights. It provides diners with exquisite and delectable two AA rosette cuisine, which is coupled with one of the finest and most diverse wine cellars in the region.
A treasure trove of fine wines and rare vintages managed by the resident sommelier, means diners can select the ideal bottle to complement their meal.

At the helm of the kitchen is French-born head chef, Loic Gratadoux. After studying at the École Supérieure de Cuisine Française, Loic spent two years at La Table du Lancaster in Paris before travelling to Australia to chef in one of the finest seafood restaurants, Pier, in Sydney. He now heads a nine-strong brigade of creative and talented chefs. The kitchen is supplied with the freshest of ingredients from the region and their food is a creative and exciting combination of classic British fare with a French twist.

Loic is passionate about ingredients. He believes in using only the finest, hand-sourced local produce, and has befriended many local fishermen and farmers. His policy is simple: if food is not fresh and not in season, it's not on the menu.

Relish Restaurant Rewards
See page 003 for details.

Harbour Heights is the crown jewel of a family-owned collection of four individual and stylish hotels, all idyllically positioned along Poole and Bournemouth's stunning coast. With its boutique style and intimate attention to detail, Harbour Heights is contemporary elegance at its very best.

The breathtaking views are unique. The south-facing teak-decked terrace takes advantage of the sun all year round and is perfect for a leisurely alfresco meal or sunset drinks with good company.

SCALLOPS WITH ROMANESCO BROCCOLI, CAULIFLOWER DUO & HAZELNUT DRESSING

SERVES 4

🍷 *Châteauneuf-du-Pape Blanc, Château de Beaucastel 2009 (Rhone, France)*

Ingredients

12 hand-dived scallops (in their shells)
1 orange cauliflower
1 romanesco broccoli
1 bunch pencil leeks

Cauliflower Purée

1 cauliflower
milk (to cover)
double cream (dash of)
salt (pinch of)

Hazelnut Dressing

50g whole hazelnuts (*blanched*)
3 shallots (finely diced)
35g walnut vinegar
60ml extra virgin olive oil
salt and pepper (to season)

Method

For The Scallops

Start by opening the scallops. This is done by inserting a knife into the shell and scraping it along the inside of the flat top of the shell. Once open, remove only the white part of the scallop from the base and keep them on the side until needed.

For The Purée

Bring a pan of milk to the boil. Cut the cauliflower into small slices and add them to the milk. Gently simmer until the cauliflower is soft. At this point, discard the milk and place the cauliflower in a blender. Add to this the dash of double cream and salt, then blend until smooth.

For The Vegetables

Cut the orange cauliflower and romanesco broccoli into small florets and trim the pencil leeks. Bring a pan of salted water to the boil, then cook the cauliflower and broccoli for 3 minutes, and the leeks for 1 minute. Transfer into ice-cold water and keep in the fridge until 30 minutes before you are ready to serve.

> **Chef's Tip**
>
> It is important to serve the vegetables and purée at room temperature. If they are too cold then the flavours will not shine.

For The Hazelnut Dressing

Preheat the oven to 180°C before roasting the hazelnuts for 3 minutes. Take them out and slightly crush them, leaving rough pieces. Mix with the shallots, salt, pepper, walnut vinegar and the olive oil.

To Serve

Start by laying the cauliflower purée on the plate before adding the vegetables. Heat a frying pan to a high temperature, then panfry the scallops for 1 minute, searing them on each side. Transfer these to the plate and generously drizzle with the hazelnut dressing.

BLACK & WHITE WHITING WITH SQUID INK GNOCCHI

SERVES 4

 Beaune Clos des Mouches, Joseph Drouhin 2008
(Burgundy, France)

Ingredients

4 x 125g (minimum) fillets whiting (skin on)

Purée

1 small celeriac
milk (to cover)
double cream (dash of)

Squid Ink Sauce

2 medium onions (finely diced)
1 tbsp olive oil
1 large beef tomato
4 x 3g sachets squid ink
salt (pinch of)

Gnocchi

1kg large baking potatoes
2 medium egg yolks
120g plain flour
3 x 3g sachets squid ink
50g Parmesan cheese (grated)

Squid Ink Crackling

800ml water
250g tapioca
15ml fish sauce
10g squid ink

Garnish

1 shimeji mushroom
1 lemon (juice of)
olive oil (dash of)
salt (pinch of)

Chef's Tip

When taking the fish off the heat, add a little knob of butter to cool down the pan and keep the fish nice and juicy at the same time.

Method

For The Celeriac Purée

Bring a pan of milk to boil. Peel the celeriac and cut into small chunks, before adding to the milk and simmering until soft. Once soft, discard the milk and place the celeriac in a blender with a dash of double cream. Blend until smooth. Add a touch more cream if necessary to get your desired consistency. Transfer to the fridge and keep covered until needed.

For The Squid Ink Sauce

Cook the onions in the olive oil for 10 minutes, without browning. Roughly chop the tomato and add to the pan with a pinch of salt. Cook with the onions for a further 10 minutes, making sure that the onions do not colour and become too soft. Transfer to a blender, add the 4 sachets of squid ink and blend until smooth.

For The Gnocchi

Preheat the oven to 160°C and bake the potatoes for 90 minutes. During this time, mix together the egg yolks, plain flour, 3 sachets of squid ink and the grated Parmesan.

When the potatoes are soft and cooked, remove the skin and pass the potato through a mouli. Gently mix it into the egg yolk mixture with your hands. Once you have a good ball of mixture, roll to create a sausage shape and then cut into 3cm lengths. Bring a pan of water to the boil, add the gnocchi chunks and cook for 3 minutes. Once cooked, leave to cool before placing in the fridge on a clean, dry tea towel until you are ready to serve.

For The Squid Ink Crackling

Bring the 800ml of water to the boil in a pan. Place all the ingredients in the pan and simmer slowly for 40 minutes until the tapioca is tender. Then take half of the mixture and blend until smooth before returning to the pan and gently mixing. Preheat the oven to 90°C. Smear a thin layer of the mix onto baking paper and dry in the oven for 90 minutes. When dry, cut the layer into rough pieces and deep fry for 1 minute.

To Serve

Peel the shimeji mushroom and leave to marinate for 10 minutes in the olive oil, salt and lemon juice. Preheat a frying pan and fry the whiting, skin-side down, for 3 minutes, then flip them over and take the pan off the heat. Finally, re-heat the purée and ink sauce and panfry the gnocchi for 1 minute.

Serve as pictured.

LEMON & LIME CHEESECAKE WITH AN EXOTIC FRUIT SALSA

SERVES 6

 Paul Cluver Late Harvest Riesling 2011
(Elgin, South Africa)

Ingredients

Stock Syrup
250g sugar, 250ml water

Biscuit Base
100g butter
250g digestive biscuits
40g caster sugar

Cheesecake
180ml double cream
1 vanilla pod (halved lengthways)
5 egg yolks
50g sugar
1 leaf gelatine (soaked)
2 lemons and 2 limes (juice and zest of)
360g cream cheese
20g butter (softened)

Lime Jelly
5 limes (juice and zest of)
250ml water
3 leaves gelatine (soaked)
250ml stock syrup

Exotic Fruit Salsa
½ pineapple
1 ripe mango
3 passion fruits
½ red chilli (de-seeded)
50ml stock syrup
½ bunch coriander

Tuile Biscuit
170g plain flour
180g icing sugar
6 egg whites
125g butter

Garnish
micro coriander

30cm x 12cm, loose bottomed cake tin

Method

For The Stock Syrup
Place 250g of sugar and 250ml of water into a pan and dissolve slowly over a low heat. Do not allow the syrup to boil until all the sugar has dissolved, then simmer for 5 minutes. Set aside until required.

For The Biscuit Base
Melt the butter, then pour into a blender with the biscuits and sugar and blend until smooth. Press the mixture down into the base of a 30cm x 12cm loose bottomed cake tin and place in the fridge.

For The Cheesecake
First, make a crème anglaise by bringing the double cream to the boil in a pan and adding the open vanilla pod. Beat the egg yolks with the sugar before adding it to the boiling cream, slowly, whilst constantly mixing. Keep cooking until the mix thickens and coats the back of the spoon. At this point, add the soaked gelatine leaf.

Mix the juice and zest of the limes and lemons together with the cream cheese, then whisk in the butter and the crème anglaise until smooth. Pour this into the cake tin over the biscuit layer, taking care to leave room at the top for the lime jelly later. Place in the fridge to set.

For The Lime Jelly
Mix the lime juice and zest with the water and bring to simmering point in a pan. Add the soaked gelatine along with the cold stock syrup into the lime juice pan. Take the pan off the heat and pass through a fine sieve, allow the mix to cool. Once cold, pour the mix on top of the cheesecake and return to the fridge to set.

For The Exotic Fruit Salsa
Finely dice the pineapple, mango, chilli and passion fruits. Remove the coriander stalks and finely chop the leaves before mixing everything into the stock syrup.

For The Tuile Biscuit
Preheat the oven to 170°C. Sieve the flour and icing sugar into the egg white. Melt the butter and add to the mixture, whisk everything together. With a spatula, place thin layers of the mixture onto a baking tray and bake for 4-5 minutes.

To Serve
Serve as pictured.

> **Chef's Tip**
> When you cut the cheesecake, dip the knife in hot water to ensure a clean cut and deliver a beautiful finish.

100
LANGMANS
RESTAURANT

3 Church Street, Callington, Cornwall, PL17 7RE

01579 384 933
www.langmansrestaurant.co.uk

There are many reasons to visit the Tamar Valley. Not only is the Cornwall and Devon border an Area of Outstanding Natural Beauty and a World Heritage site, it is also the location of hidden gem, Langmans Restaurant in Callington. This two AA rosette restaurant offers fine dining in a warm atmosphere. Langmans has developed an enviable reputation as the place to go for an excellent dining experience, and is acknowledged as one of the best restaurants in south east Cornwall. Situated in a Grade II listed building, it nestles in the shadow of the 15th Century church of St Mary's.

Chef and owner, Anton Buttery, and his wife Gail, consistently offer excellent food at good value for money, in a friendly and relaxed setting. An evening at Langmans is planned to enable you to enjoy excellent food in an unhurried way. It begins with drinks and canapés seated on comfortable sofas in the lounge, followed by dining in the intimate restaurant.

Gail and Anton achieved their dream of owning a restaurant in 2000, and have since created the perfect setting in which to relax and enjoy the seven course Tasting Menu, which includes fresh fish, locally sourced meat, a large selection of regional cheeses and two exquisite puddings. A great deal of thought is given to how the combination of ingredients will look on the plate and taste on the palate. The tasting menu changes regularly, using ingredients from local suppliers. Such is their dedication to using fresh ingredients they grow some vegetables which are usually difficult to find.

Customers enjoy Anton's balanced menu and may have a flight of six wines with their meal or choose from a selection of over 100.

Relish Restaurant Rewards
See page 003 for details.

Langmans photography Ron Bushell Photography

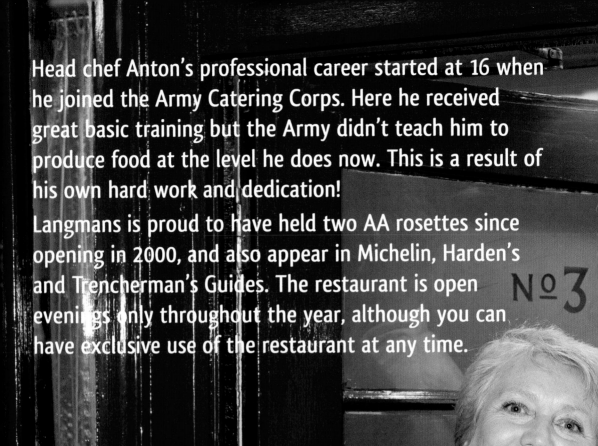

Head chef Anton's professional career started at 16 when he joined the Army Catering Corps. Here he received great basic training but the Army didn't teach him to produce food at the level he does now. This is a result of his own hard work and dedication!

Langmans is proud to have held two AA rosettes since opening in 2000, and also appear in Michelin, Harden's and Trencherman's Guides. The restaurant is open evenings only throughout the year, although you can have exclusive use of the restaurant at any time.

SCALLOPS WITH CRAB RISOTTO, SWEETCORN PUREE & CRISP BACON

SERVES 4

🍷 *Muscadet de Sevre et Maine Sur Lie, Grande Reserve, 2010, Fruitière (France)*

Ingredients

Scallops

6 large scallops (halved down the centre)
4 slices thin streaky bacon
oil (for frying)
sea salt

Crab Risotto

50g arborio rice
50g unsalted butter
25g leek (finely diced)
50ml white wine
500ml vegetable stock
100g white crabmeat (picked)
1 tomato (peeled, deseeded and diced)
½ lemon (juice of)

Sweetcorn Purée

1 cob sweetcorn
25g unsalted butter

Garnish

reserved corn kernels (cooked and toasted)
micro herbs

Method

For The Sweetcorn Purée

Hold the cob upright on a chopping board and run a sharp knife down the length to remove the kernels. Reserve some for garnishing, place the rest in a food processor and blitz until you have a purée. Strain through a sieve, pushing as much through as you can. Pour into a small pan and warm through slowly, it will thicken quite a lot. Remove from the heat and leave to one side. When ready to serve, whisk in the butter and season with some salt. If it is too thick, add a little water to get the right consistency.

For The Crab Risotto

Bring the vegetable stock to a simmer in a saucepan. Meanwhile, melt 25g of butter in another pan and add the leeks. Cook for a minute or two until soft, without colouring. Add the rice and cook for a minute. Pour in the white wine and stir until it is absorbed. Add the vegetable stock ladle by ladle and keep stirring until each is absorbed and the rice is cooked, about 12-15 minutes. It should have a creamy consistency.

Add the picked white crabmeat and tomatoes, stir through and season with salt and pepper. When ready to serve, add the remaining 25g of butter and lemon juice.

For The Bacon

Preheat the oven to 160°C. Spread the bacon out flat on a tray lined with parchment paper, top with some more paper and another tray and place in the oven for 15 minutes until golden and crisp.

For The Scallops

Heat a non-stick frying pan on a medium heat and add a little oil. When the oil is hot, add the scallops, cut side down and fry for between 30 seconds and a minute, depending on size, until golden. Turn over and cook for the same time. Remove from the pan and set aside on some kitchen paper.

To Serve

Put some of the sweetcorn purée on a hot plate and spread it slightly, spoon on three small piles of the crab risotto, place a scallop half on each with a piece of crispy bacon, scatter around some of the toasted corn kernels and a few micro herbs.

Chef's Tip

Use hand-dived scallops if possible and be sure not to overcook them!

LOIN OF LAMB WITH RED WINE SAUCE, CELERIAC PUREE, NEW POTATOES, GIROLLES & BABY LEEKS

SERVES 4

 Bethany Grenache 2006 (Australia)

Ingredients

2 x 300g lamb loin (trimmed)
100g small new potatoes
8 baby leeks
oil and butter (for frying)
sea salt and black pepper (to season)

Red Wine Sauce

350ml red wine
50ml port
350ml chicken stock
1 sprig rosemary
1 star anise
1 tbsp redcurrant jelly
sherry vinegar (dash of)
15g unsalted butter (cold)

Celeriac Purée

1 celeriac (peeled and cut into 1cm dice)
50g unsalted butter
125ml double cream
ground white pepper (to season)

Girolles

100g girolles
25g butter
Madeira or sherry (dash of)

Garnish

12 chantenay carrots
romanesco cauliflower florets

Chef's Tip

Turn your leftover celeriac purée into a lunch time treat by adding some milk to thin it down a little and reheating. Enjoy with some crusty bread!

Method

For The Red Wine Sauce

Bring the red wine to a simmer in a small saucepan and reduce by half. Add the port, chicken stock, rosemary, star anise, redcurrant jelly, some black pepper and reduce by half again. Strain through a fine sieve into a clean saucepan, add a dash of sherry vinegar and whisk in the cold butter.

For The Celeriac Purée

Put the diced celeriac into a saucepan with half of the butter and a sprinkling of salt. Cover and gently cook on the hob. When tender, add 75ml of the double cream and cook without the lid for another minute or two, then pour into a food processor, add the rest of the butter and the cream and blitz to a purée. Pass through a sieve and season.

For The Girolles

Ensure there is no grit on your mushrooms. Heat a frying pan and add the butter. When it is hot, add the girolles. Cook for a minute or two then add a dash of Madeira and a pinch of sea salt. Remove from the heat and keep warm. If you can't find girolles use small oyster mushrooms instead.

For The New Potatoes And Vegetables

Cover the new potatoes in a pan with cold salted water, bring to the boil and simmer until tender.

Take the outer leaves off the leeks and trim to size. Heat a small pan with a little water and some unsalted butter. When it comes to the boil, add the leeks and simmer until tender. Repeat with the carrots and cauliflower.

For The Lamb Loin

Heat an ovenproof frying pan until hot, add a little oil and fry the loins until browned. Season with sea salt and black pepper then place in the oven at around 160°C for 7-8 minutes. Remove from the oven and allow the lamb to rest, in a clean pan which is covered.

To Serve

Put a good couple of teaspoons of celeriac purée on hot plates towards the bottom left side and then spread with a palette knife towards the opposite side. Arrange the potatoes, leeks, other vegetables and girolles on the celeriac purée. Carve the lamb loin in half lengthways and then in half the other way. Place next to the vegetables. Pour any juices from the lamb into the red wine sauce, then drizzle this around the lamb and serve.

CHOCOLATE TART WITH PISTACHIO ICE CREAM, HONEYCOMB, 100s & 1000s

SERVES 4

 Tokaji Aszu 5 Puttonyos 2002, Crown Estates (Hungary)

Ingredients

Sweet Pastry

110g unsalted butter (cubed)
70g icing sugar (sieved)
25g ground hazelnuts
25g ground almonds
salt (pinch of)
1 egg (beaten)
165g plain flour (sieved)

Chocolate Filling

150ml whipping cream
20g Demerara sugar
170g dark chocolate (finely chopped)
25g unsalted butter (room temperature, cubed)

Honeycomb

75g caster sugar, 25ml glucose syrup
15ml honey
4g bicarbonate of soda

100s And 1000s

10g chocolate covered popping candy
10g freeze dried raspberry pieces
10g green pistachio nuts (chopped)
10g honeycomb pieces (chopped)

Pistachio Ice Cream

300ml full-fat milk, 200ml double cream
5 large egg yolks
115g caster sugar
125g green pistachio nuts (peeled)
natural green food colouring (dash of)

Caramel Hazelnuts

8 hazelnuts (whole, peeled)
100g caster sugar, 1 tbsp water

Garnish

fresh raspberries

4 x 7cm tart moulds

Method

For The Sweet Pastry

Beat the butter and icing sugar together in a mixing bowl until light in colour. Mix in the ground nuts and the salt. Beat until smooth. Gradually add the egg. Lastly, add the flour and mix to form a smooth dough. Wrap in clingfilm and chill for at least 1 hour. Roll the pastry out thinly and line 4 tart moulds, letting the pastry hang over the sides. Bake at 180ºC for 15 minutes. After 5 minutes check for any bubbles in the pastry and press down to squash them. Allow to cool then trim the edges.

For The Chocolate Filling

Place the chocolate and butter in a bowl. Put the cream and Demerara sugar in a saucepan and bring to the boil. Gradually add the cream to the chocolate and butter until fully combined. Cover and set aside, but don't place in the fridge.

> **Chef's Tip**
> Transfer any leftover chocolate filling to the fridge. Once set, scoop into balls, roll in some cocoa powder and serve as petit fours with coffee.

For The Honeycomb

Line a small tray with some baking parchment. Put the caster sugar, glucose and honey into a pan with a tablespoon of water and heat until it reaches 150ºC or turns golden brown. Tip in the bicarbonate of soda and mix - it will start to bubble. Pour straight into the tray and allow to cool. Break into pieces.

For The Pistachio Ice Cream

Whisk together the egg yolks and 65g of caster sugar in a bowl, set aside. Put the milk, cream and 50g of caster sugar into a pan and bring to the boil, pour half into the egg yolks, whisking as you do so, and pour back into the pan. Lower the heat and stir until it coats the back of a spoon (85ºC). Remove from the heat, pour half into a food processor with 75g of the pistachios and blitz. Return to the pan, add food colouring as desired then cool. Chop the remaining pistachios, saving half for the garnish. Churn in an ice cream machine, adding the pistachios near the end of the process. If you don't have an ice cream machine see page 231.

Caramel Hazelnuts

Put the caster sugar and water in a small pan and heat until it turns golden brown. Place the bottom of the pan in cold water to stop the caramel going any darker. Dip the hazelnuts, skewered with cocktail stick, into the caramel and hang from a shelf. Allow to cool and cut to length.

To Serve

Fill the pastry cases with the chocolate filling. Mix the 100s and 1000s ingredients together in a bowl and sprinkle over the chocolate filling. Spoon a little of the chocolate filling on the plate and place the tart on top so it doesn't slide around. Arrange the other elements of this dish as pictured.

110
LUCKNAM PARK

Colerne, Chippenham, Wiltshire, SN14 8AZ

01225 742 777
www.lucknampark.co.uk

A chef does not earn and maintain a Michelin star for ten years without first having learnt his craft at some of the finest restaurants in the UK, and this is so very true for Hywel Jones. His back catalogue includes Chez Nico, Marco Pierre White, Foliage at the Mandarin Oriental and the Pharmacy in Notting Hill. Michelin stars glitter all over his CV.

"I have been executive head chef at Lucknam Park since 2004 and during this time I have worked hard to keep the food offering moving forward, not just in The Park, our fine dining restaurant but also in the more contemporary Brasserie. The Michelin star is what sets the standard across every dining experience we offer but ultimately we look to serve good food that always demonstrates the best of the local and seasonal produce that is in abundance in the south west.

In late 2012, after years of planning, we opened the Cookery School at Lucknam Park. This has been a whole new challenge and those who know me know that whilst I love being in the kitchen, being in front of an audience is a bit more daunting! The school is headed up on a daily basis by Hrishikesh Desai who loves to be up front and is a real star in there. For me I have to step out of my comfort zone and get involved; I love sharing my skills and passing my passion for food and my belief in provenance and food quality on to the guests and interacting with them on such a personal level. It's a new challenge and challenges are what keep me cooking and loving what I do."
Executive Head Chef, Hywel Jones.

Relish Restaurant Rewards
See page 003 for details.

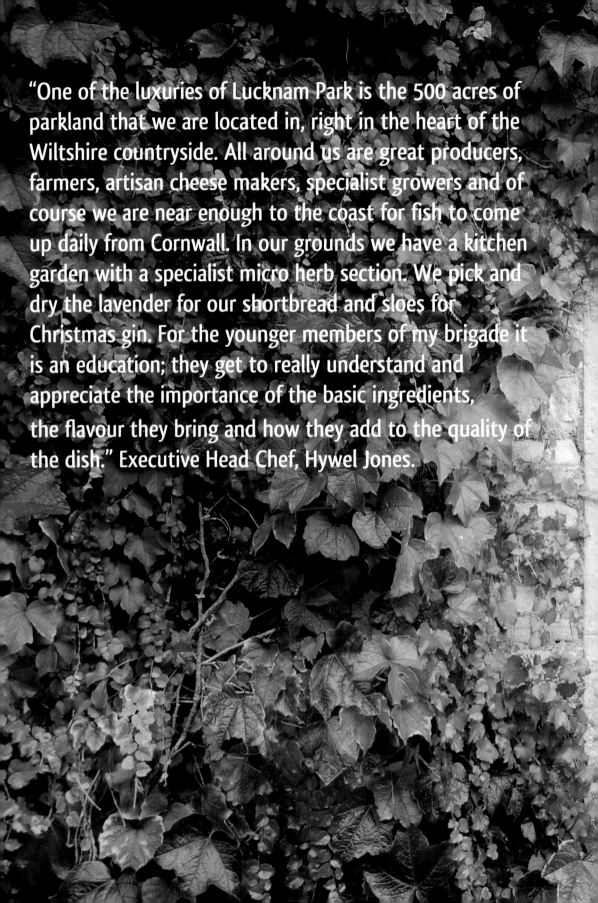

"One of the luxuries of Lucknam Park is the 500 acres of parkland that we are located in, right in the heart of the Wiltshire countryside. All around us are great producers, farmers, artisan cheese makers, specialist growers and of course we are near enough to the coast for fish to come up daily from Cornwall. In our grounds we have a kitchen garden with a specialist micro herb section. We pick and dry the lavender for our shortbread and sloes for Christmas gin. For the younger members of my brigade it is an education; they get to really understand and appreciate the importance of the basic ingredients,

the flavour they bring and how they add to the quality of the dish." Executive Head Chef, Hywel Jones.

SLOW COOKED SIRLOIN OF DEVONSHIRE ROSE VEAL, SWEETBREADS GLAZED IN PANCETTA, MARINATED SALSIFY, TRUFFLE VINAIGRETTE

SERVES 4

 Albariño Leirana 2010, Finca Genoveva, Forjas del Salnés, Rias Baixas (Spain)

Ingredients

1kg piece veal loin (fat and sinew removed)

Marinated Salsify
10 spears salsify (peeled, sliced into ribbons)
50ml white wine
50ml white wine vinegar, 50ml virgin oil olive
1 shallot (finely chopped)
2 black peppercorns

Sweetbread Boudins
250g veal sweetbreads
plain flour (to dust), salt and pepper (to season)
8-10 slices pancetta (thinly sliced)
chicken jus (to glaze, optional)
butter (to glaze)

Chicken Mousseline
1 chicken breast (skinless), ½ egg white
22ml double cream, salt (to season)

Girolles
200g baby girolles (cleaned), 1 shallot (*brunoise*)
1 sprig tarragon (left whole)
salt and pepper (to season)

Vinaigrette (combine all ingredients)
1 tbsp Chardonnay vinegar
3 tbsp olive oil, ¼ tsp Dijon mustard
½ tsp boiling water, salt (pinch of)

Truffle Vinaigrette
2 egg yolks, 50ml sherry vinegar
50ml reduced truffle *jus* (from tinned truffles)
300ml groundnut oil
truffle oil (to taste), honey (to taste)

Garnish
micro shoots
truffle (half sliced, half grated, optional)

Method

For The Veal Loin
Cut lengthways into 3 or 4 pieces and trim into neat cylinders. Clingfilm tightly to retain shape, sous vide and poach at 58°C in a water bath for roughly 40 minutes. Blast chill and set aside.

Alternatively, wrap in clingfilm to form a cylinder, tie tightly at both ends and poach in a pan of water (58-60°C) for 30 minutes. Refresh in a bowl of iced water for 20 minutes.

For The Mousseline
Blend the chicken breast with the egg white and a pinch of salt. Pass through a drum sieve and gradually beat in the cream over ice.

For The Sweetbread Boudins
Soak, *blanch* and peel the sweetbreads. Break into 2.5cm nuggets and dust lightly in seasoned flour. Panfry until golden but still underdone. Chill and mix with the mousseline (just enough to bind). Roll in clingfilm into long cylinders, the diameter of a 2p piece, and then poach at 75°C until cooked. Remove from the clingfilm, wrap in the pancetta and cut into 2.5cm pieces.

For The Marinated Salsify
Bring all the ingredients to a boil, pour over the salsify ribbons and leave overnight.

For The Girolles
Soften the shallot in a little olive oil, add the girolles and tarragon. Cook briefly, remove from the heat, season and dress with the vinaigrette.

For The Truffle Vinaigrette
Whisk together the egg yolks, vinegar and truffle *jus* in a food processor. With the motor running, slowly trickle in the groundnut oil until it *emulsifies*. Add the truffle oil and honey to taste and mix well.

To Serve
Slice 3 neat rounds of veal, glaze with a little olive oil and season, then arrange evenly around a plate. Panfry the sweetbread boudins, using a little chicken *jus* and butter to glaze, and place in the middle of the plate. Arrange the girolles and salsify ribbons around and add a few drops of truffle vinaigrette. Finish with some micro shoots plus grated and sliced truffle.

POT ROAST GROUSE, SAVOY CABBAGE, CHANTERELLES & ELDERBERRIES

SERVES 4

🍷 *Post Scriptum de Chryseia 2010, Douro Valley (Portugal)*

Ingredients

Grouse

4 grouse (oven ready)
200ml duck fat
sea salt

Sauce

50g *mirepoix*
200ml red wine
100ml port
400ml brown game stock
1 sprig thyme
1 bay leaf
3 juniper berries
3 black peppercorns
50ml elderflower liqueur
2 tbsp elderberries

½ Savoy cabbage
100g chanterelles
200g mashed potato (dry)
100g unsalted butter
50ml milk
1 large chipping potato
oil (to deep fry)

Method

For The Grouse (Prepare 24 hours in advance)

Remove the legs from the grouse and cure lightly in sea salt for 24 hours. Rinse, pat dry and cook slowly in the duck fat in a moderate oven (180°C) for around 2 hours, or until the meat falls away from the bone easily. Allow to cool, flake and discard any bone, sinews or skin. Remove wishbones and winglets from the remaining carcass, leaving the breasts attached, and chop finely.

For The Sauce

Gently caramelise the grouse trimmings along with the *mirepoix*. Remove from pan, add the port and wine and reduce by two thirds. Add the stock, bring to the boil and add the trimmings back to the pan, along with the herbs and spices. Simmer gently for 30 minutes, skimming frequently. *Flambé* the elderflower liqueur and add to the sauce. Pass through a muslin cloth and set aside.

For The Cabbage

Remove the outer leaves from the cabbage. Cut 8 neat 8cm wide discs from the best leaves. Remove the stalk from the remaining cabbage and shred finely.

For The Potatoes

Heat the dry mash and whisk in the butter and milk. Season, pass through a fine sieve and then pour into a gas syphon. Seal and charge with gas. Keep warm in a water bath. Alternatively, return to a clean pan, cover and keep warm.

Peel the chipping potato and, using a *mandolin*, cut into strings. Carefully wrap around a metal tube to form a cylinder and deep fry until golden brown. Make 4.

To Serve

Roast the grouse in a moderate oven around 180°C for roughly 6 minutes. Allow to rest before removing the breasts from the carcass. The meat should be slightly pink.

Cook the cabbage discs in a little butter *emulsion* and place 2 per serving plate and top with a potato ring. Sweat the shredded cabbage and chanterelles in a little butter, season and mix in the flaked leg meat. Place this mixture inside the potato rings. Sit the grouse breasts in front of potato ring. Reduce the sauce to the required consistency and stir in the elderberries. Pipe the potato mousse into the rings and dress the grouse breasts with the sauce.

BITTER CHOCOLATE & HAZELNUT BAR, CANNELLONI OF ROAST APPLE, CANDIED HAZELNUT ICE CREAM

SERVES 4

🍷 *Coteaux de l'Aubance, Domaine de Montgilet 2010, Les Trois Schistes, Loire Valley (France)*

Ingredients

Cannelloni Mix
250g sugar
75g ground almonds
60g plain flour
90ml apple juice
125g butter (melted)

Dark Chocolate Mousse
150g dark chocolate (at least 55% cocoa)
40g sugar, 20ml water
4 egg yolks
190ml whipping cream (whipped to soft peaks)

Hazelnut Sponge
55g icing sugar
55g ground hazelnuts
3 egg yolks, 1 whole egg
80g plain flour (sieved)
4 egg whites, 55g sugar
35g butter (melted, then cooled)

Apple Jelly
4 red apples (peeled and roughly chopped)
40g butter
125g sugar
250ml apple juice
25ml calvados
2 leaves gelatine (soaked in water)

Candied Hazelnut Ice Cream
200g caster sugar
125g hazelnuts
375ml full-fat milk
120ml double cream
25g milk powder
1 vanilla pod (seeds scraped out)
2 egg yolks

33cm x 25cm Swiss roll tin (greased and lined)

Method

For The Cannelloni
Combine all the ingredients and mix until smooth. Refrigerate, then spread thinly onto a non-stick mat. Bake at 180°C until golden. Cool slightly, cut into 8cm x 6cm rectangles and roll around a whisk handle to make tubes. Leave to set. Make 4.

For The Dark Chocolate Mousse
Melt chocolate over a *bain marie*. Heat the sugar in a separate pan to 121°C with the water. Whisk the egg yolks until they have doubled in volume, then slowly add the cooked sugar, whisking constantly until the mixture is just warm. Mix with the chocolate and fold in the cream.

For The Hazelnut Sponge
Beat together the icing sugar, hazelnuts, whole egg and egg yolks until smooth, about 10-15 minutes. Fold in the flour.

Whip the egg whites into medium peaks with the sugar. Mix one third of the egg whites with the hazelnut mixture, then fold in the remaining egg whites. Add the butter, spread onto trays and cook at 170°C for 8-10 minutes.

To Make The Chocolate Bar
Sandwich the chocolate mousse between the sponge sheets and repeat to a height of around 2.5cm. Press gently with a flat tray and then allow to set in the fridge. Cut into bars of 8cm x 2cm. Dust in cocoa powder or spray dark chocolate using an air gun.

For The Apple Jelly (Prepare the day before)
Gently melt the sugar without stirring. Add the butter, calvados and apples. Cook on a low heat for 15-20 minutes then add the apple juice. Keep in the fridge overnight. Strain the apples, then set the liquid with the gelatine to 1cm thick. Cube. Crush the apples and reserve. Place in the cannelloni just prior to serving.

For The Candied Hazelnut Ice Cream
Gently melt 40g of sugar without stirring, then add the hazelnuts. Leave to cool. Boil the milk and cream. Crush the hazelnuts and add, clingfilm, leave for 30 minutes.

Pass through a sieve into a fresh pan and bring back to the boil. Add the milk powder, 100g of sugar and vanilla seeds. Simmer for 2 minutes. Blend.

Whisk the egg yolks and 60g of caster sugar together and pour a small amount of the flavoured milk onto it. Add back to the pan, cook on a low heat, stirring frequently, until it coats the back of a spoon (82°C). Remove from the heat. Pour into a bowl set over ice. When cooled, churn in an ice cream machine, or see page 231.

To Serve
Serve as pictured.

120
THE MASONS ARMS

Knowstone, South Molton, Devon, EX36 4RY

01398 341 231
www.masonsarmsdevon.co.uk

The Masons Arms has been a hostelry in Knowstone since the 13th Century, and we have been the proud custodians since 2005 when we made a life changing decision to set up in Devon. Having spent 18 years cooking side by side with Michel Roux as his head chef at The Waterside Inn, I was anxious to put all of that experience to the test. Our template was to make the pub exactly the kind of place that we would like to find if exploring Devon, with friendly service and first class food.

I run the kitchen with my team of local chefs and my wife Sarah expertly looks after our customers' needs with her team. We are still very much the village local with a first class pint and with the help of the internet we are a global local!

Our location is in the rolling foothills of Exmoor but our reputation has spread beyond the county boundaries, and we are a great stop off for foodie visitors on their way to North Cornwall.

We take great pride in our menus and wine list and try to use local ingredients as much as possible as, after all, we are surrounded with fabulous produce. Local game is a speciality in season, as is fabulous fresh fish from both of Devon's coasts and of course the Red Ruby Devon beef!
Mark Dodson, Owner and Chef

Relish Restaurant Rewards
See page 003 for details.

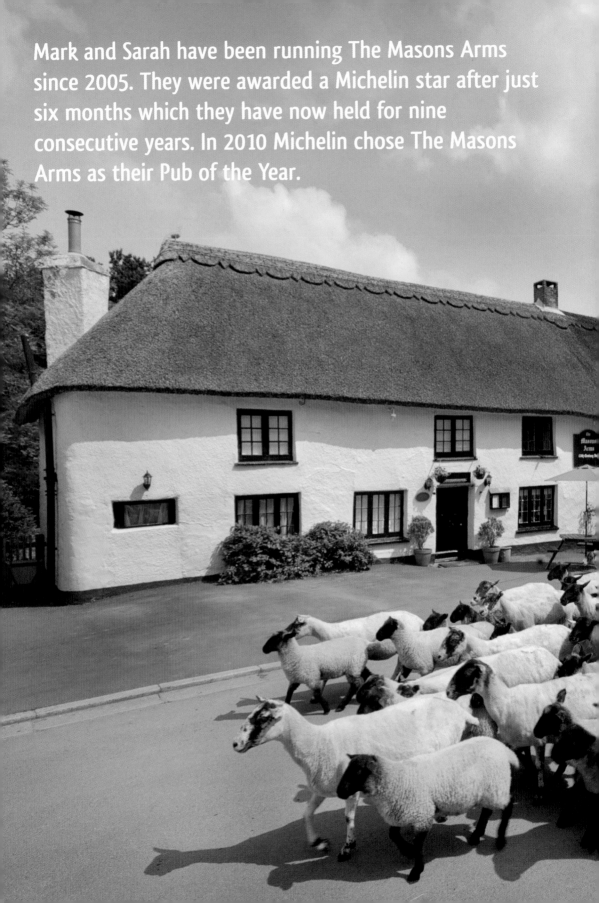

Mark and Sarah have been running The Masons Arms since 2005. They were awarded a Michelin star after just six months which they have now held for nine consecutive years. In 2010 Michelin chose The Masons Arms as their Pub of the Year.

Mark's impressive background is the starting point for his cooking and he and his young team create menus using the finest local and seasonal produce. A first class pub serving first class food, truly two experiences in one!

SEARED SCALLOPS WITH PEAR & VANILLA

SERVES 4

 Esporão Reserva Branco, Alentejo (Portugal)

Ingredients

12 large scallops

Poached Pears

3 pears
150ml red wine
150g sugar

Lime Cream

50g soft cream cheese
½ lime (juice and zest of)

Vanilla Sauce

1 shallot (finely chopped)
25ml Noilly Prat
60ml double cream
1 coral (optional, retained from the scallops)
4 drops excellent quality vanilla extract
(with the seeds)

salad and herbs (to garnish)

Method

For The Pears

Peel and slice the pears with the aid of a *mandolin* to get 12 long slices and 12 x 3cm discs. Remove any seeds and core from the long slices. Bring the wine and sugar to the boil and then add the pear slices and discs. Cook for 1-2 minutes, depending on the ripeness of the pears. If left for up to 24 hours, the pears will take on a lovely burgundy colour.

> **Chef's Tip**
>
> Keep all of the pear trimmings and cook them with a little sugar, vanilla and water to make a purée to garnish the plates.

For The Vanilla Sauce

Cook the shallot and Noilly Prat in a pan and, when almost dry, add the cream. Simmer gently until the sauce thickens. Pass through a fine sieve and reserve. To add an extra richness, a scallop coral can be dropped into the warm sauce, blended, and re-passed through the sieve. Finish the sauce with the vanilla extract and season.

For The Lime Cream

Mix the lime juice and zest thoroughly with the cream cheese.

To Serve

Dress each plate with three slices of pear. In the centre of each pear add a touch of the lime cream. Sear the scallops in a smoking hot pan until they are slightly hot to the touch. Place a scallop in the centre of each pear, add a little of the pear purée to each plate and lightly sauce the dish. Top each of the scallops with a circle of the poached pear and garnish with a little salad and herbs.

BREAST OF WOOD PIGEON WITH BLUEBERRY JUS

SERVES 4

🍷 *Lirac Clos de Sixte, Alain Jaume & Fils, Rhone (France)*

Ingredients

8 wood pigeon breasts (skinned)
1 large potato
olive oil (to fry)

Beetroot Purée

300g raw beetroot (peeled and roughly chopped)
25g soft dark brown sugar
50ml red wine vinegar
200ml double cream

Blueberry Jus

50g blueberries
50g caster sugar
50ml red wine vinegar
100ml dark chicken or veal stock

Garnish

100g picked salad leaves
1 red apple (sliced *julienne*)
wild mushrooms

Method

For The Beetroot Purée

Cook the beetroot in a pan of water with a pinch of salt until soft. Once cooked, drain well and return to the pan. Stir the pieces round to evaporate the last of the liquid. Cook a little with the soft dark brown sugar and then pour in the red wine vinegar. Cook further until the liquid is a nice caramel colour and then add the double cream. Leave to cook and thicken. Place the mixture into a blender and blend until smooth, season to taste. Reserve and keep hot.

For The Blueberry Jus

Keep 16 blueberries to one side and put the others in a pan with the caster sugar and the red wine vinegar and reduce. Crush the blueberries in the pan with a fork. When the liquid is syrupy, add the stock and cook further until it is a syrupy consistency again. Pass through a fine sieve and add the remaining 16 blueberries.

For The Crisps

Peel and cut the potatoes using a *mandolin* to create 'Pommes Gaufrettes' as illustrated. Rinse in water, pat dry, and then fry in hot oil until golden. Drain on absorbent paper, season and reserve until serving.

To Serve

Shallow fry the pigeon breasts in a hot pan with a little olive oil - a couple of minutes on each side will leave them pink. Leave them to rest before slicing. Place the purée onto the plate and decorate with some salad leaves, apple and wild mushrooms. Slice the pigeon and arrange on the plate, pour on the *jus* and place the potato crisps on top of the pigeon. Serve immediately.

> **Chef's Tip**
> Be sure to thoroughly check over the pigeon breasts for shot!

WHITE CHOCOLATE CHEESECAKE WITH MARINATED STRAWBERRIES & CLOTTED CREAM ICE CREAM

SERVES 4

 Cristallo Vin de Fraise, Peter Knupp, Valais (Switzerland)

Ingredients

Strawberry Jelly

20g sugar
15g strawberry purée
30ml sweet wine
¼ leaf gelatine (soaked in water)

Cheesecake

3 digestive biscuits
3 ginger nut biscuits
20g *clarified* butter
35g sugar
2 egg yolks
10ml double cream
½ leaf gelatine (soaked in water)
100g soft cream cheese (softened)
85g white chocolate (melted)
100ml cream (lightly whipped)

Clotted Cream Ice Cream

50g sugar
2 egg yolks (beaten)
100ml full-fat milk
30ml double cream
100g clotted cream

Strawberry Garnish

100g strawberries (quartered)
10g icing sugar
20ml orange juice

4 x 7cm round moulds

Method

For The Jelly

Bring the purée, wine and sugar to the boil, add the soaked gelatine and then pass through a fine sieve. Leave to cool in a fridge until almost set before using.

For The Cheesecake

Blend the biscuits in a food processor, then bind the crumbs with the *clarified* butter. Push this firmly into the moulds to form an even base.

Bring the sugar to the boil with a drop of water and pour onto the egg yolks. Whisk until pale. Warm the double cream and dissolve the gelatine into this. Add to the yolks and continue whisking until cool. Add to this the softened cream cheese, then the melted chocolate and finally the whipped cream. Spoon on top of the biscuit bases leaving a small gap for the jelly. Refrigerate until set. Once set, top with the jelly and refrigerate until needed.

For The Ice Cream

Beat together the sugar and egg yolks. Boil the milk and double cream together and pour this onto the yolks, mixing well. With a hand blender, blend in the clotted cream and leave to cool. Once cooled, churn in an ice cream maker until set, or see page 231.

For The Strawberries

Liquidise together 40g of the strawberries, the icing sugar and orange juice. Pass through a fine sieve and add the remaining 80g of quartered strawberries.

To Serve

De-mould the cheesecakes, place onto your plates and top with the marinated strawberries. Garnish the plate with lines of the strawberry marinade and serve with a generous helping of the ice cream!

Chef's Tip

Gently heat the outside of the cheesecake rings with a blow torch to remove them neatly.

130
THE MILLBROOK INN

South Pool, Kingsbridge, Devon, TQ7 2RW

01548 531 581
www.millbrookinnsouthpool.co.uk

Nestled in the pretty waterside village of south Pool at the end of a creek off the Salcombe estuary, the multi-award-winning Millbrook Inn attracts customers from across the south and west of England, with some people travelling more than a hundred miles to tuck into their legendary Sunday rib roast in front of a roaring log fire.

Owners Ian Dent and Diana Hunt never had any intention of following the herd when they took over the pub they now own.

"We came to The Millbrook with very clear ideas about what the pub should represent on the food front," says Ian. "We didn't want it to be gastro. Instead we wanted inspired country food, obviously locally sourced. Our idea was to mix up good pub grub and simple restaurant food."

Five years ago he met his present head chef, Jean-Phillipe Bidart, better known as JP. An avowed devotee of rural French 'auberge' style cooking, the classically-trained Parisian chef soon put his stamp on the venue, offering classically-inspired dishes, family recipes and the best the South Hams can offer on the meat and fish front.

Its position by the water does mean that seafood often sits prominently on the menu but not exclusively so and rarely conventionally. Bouillabaisse is the main stay, cooked the way JP's grandmother taught him (well, perhaps with one or two minor adjustments) and then there's a recent addition - Monkfish Osso Bucco, which is a wonderful conundrum of a French chef cooking an Italian inspired dish in a tiny rural English pub.

JP works with a number of local farmers who rear pigs, sheep and geese specifically for the table and the pub has invested in its own 20 acre micro-farm. This has created an extra dimension to menu planning and inevitably a greater understanding and respect for the energy required to consistently produce high quality livestock.

The Millbrook farm also supplies the local community from its veg shed, which provides fruit, vegetables, bacon and sausage and is run 24 hours a day using an honesty box. "The last remaining village store disappeared from south Pool more than ten years ago," says Diana. "Our veg shed is a practical way of reintroducing fresh produce to purchase in the village."

Relish Restaurant Rewards
See page 003 for details.

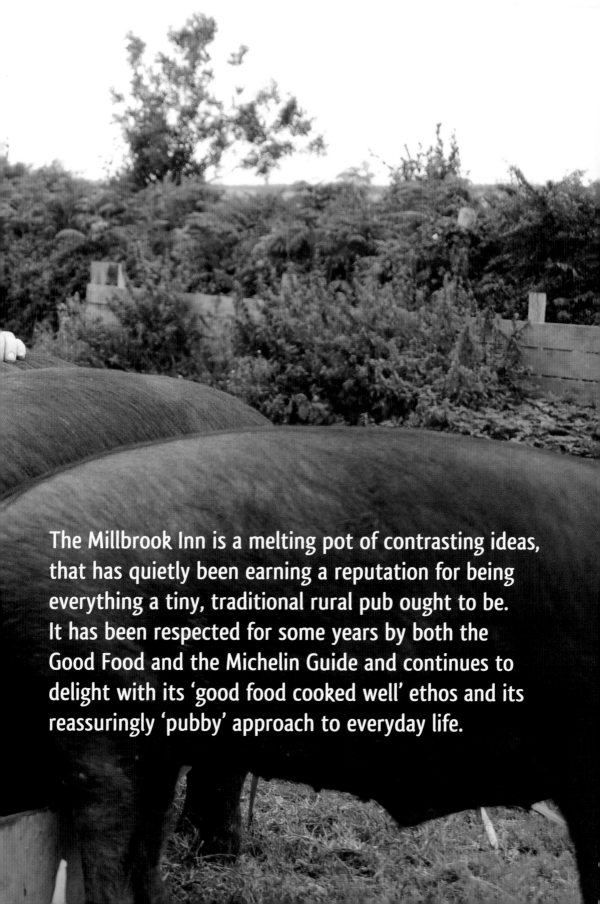

The Millbrook Inn is a melting pot of contrasting ideas, that has quietly been earning a reputation for being everything a tiny, traditional rural pub ought to be. It has been respected for some years by both the Good Food and the Michelin Guide and continues to delight with its 'good food cooked well' ethos and its reassuringly 'pubby' approach to everyday life.

ASSIETTE OF GOAT'S CHEESE

SERVES 4

 Pinot Grigio, or a soft red Syrah

Ingredients

vegetable oil (for frying)
salt and white pepper (to season)

Arancini
100g arborio rice
25g white onion (diced)
50ml white wine
1 bay leaf, 2 sprigs thyme
150ml water
60g goat's cheese (crumbled)
50g plain white flour
2 eggs (beaten)
100g Panko breadcrumbs

Beignet
120g goat's cheese (rind off)
cracked black pepper (pinch of)
50g plain white flour
2 eggs (beaten)
100g Panko breadcrumbs

Mousse
120g goat's cheese (rind off)
60ml double cream

Spiced Tomato Chutney
200g ripe tomatoes (diced)
50g red onion (diced)
½ star anise
¼ fresh red chilli (very finely sliced)
50ml red wine vinegar, 25ml red wine
25g caster sugar
salt and black pepper (to season)
1 bay leaf, 1 sprig thyme
olive oil (splash of)

Pea Purée
150g frozen peas
extra virgin olive oil (dash of)

Beetroot Pickle
100g beetroot (raw, *julienne*)
100ml red wine, 50ml balsamic vinegar
1 sprig thyme, 1 small bay leaf
25g caster sugar

Method

For The Arancini
Heat 5ml of vegetable oil in a saucepan then fry the diced onions until translucent. Add the rice, frying until it starts to become shiny. *Deglaze* with the white wine. Add the bay leaf, thyme, some salt and pepper and the water and cook slowly on the stove without stirring for 15-20 minutes. When cooked, spread out on a tray and let it get really cold.

Once cold, mix in a bowl with the crumbled goat's cheese. Season well. Divide the risotto into 4 equal balls. Carefully dredge the balls, one at a time, first in the flour then the eggs and finally the Panko breadcrumbs. Deep fry at 170°C until crisp and golden brown.

For The Beignet
Beat the goat's cheese, with some cracked black pepper, until soft. Divide into 4 equal balls, then coat in flour, egg and breadcrumbs as with the arancini. Deep fry at 170°C for about 2 minutes or until golden brown.

For The Mousse (Best prepared the day before)
Soften the goat's cheese with a Magimix, or whisk until smooth. Gently fold in some salt, pepper and the cream and place in the fridge to firm up.

For The Tomato Chutney
Sweat the red onion in a pan and then add the tomatoes, chilli, salt, pepper, bay leaf, thyme and star anise. *Deglaze* with the red wine vinegar. Add the red wine and sugar and reduce by half until the texture is similar to jam. Place it in the fridge.

For The Pea Purée
Blanch the peas in hot salted water and then refresh in ice cold water. Drain, then purée in a liquidiser or with a stick blender. Pass through a sieve, then add the extra virgin olive oil and season. Keep in the fridge.

For The Beetroot Pickle
Add all the ingredients, except the raw beetroot, to a saucepan and bring to the boil. Pour the liquid on top of the beetroot and leave to cool.

To Serve
Serve as pictured placing an arancini, beignet and mousse on a single plate with a spoonful of spiced chutney, beetroot pickle and pea purée.

Chef's Tip
Everything can be prepared the day before and it can all be made within an hour. It is better to prepare the goat's cheese mousse the day before to let it set.

BOUILLABAISSE

SERVES 6

🍷 *Sancerre - a fresh, aromatic white wine, prized by the locals in France, that matches well with fish and seafood.*

Ingredients

1.3kg locally-caught fish (see method)

Bouillabaisse

1kg fish bones with heads (see method)
20ml olive oil
3 cloves garlic
2 sticks celery
1 bulb fennel
2 carrots
1 small leek
60ml Pernod
200ml white wine
2 sprigs thyme
1 bay leaf
saffron (pinch of)
200g tomato purée
salt and black pepper (to season)

Rouille

4 cloves garlic
2 egg yolks
saffron (pinch of)
1 tsp lemon juice
100-150ml olive oil
salt (pinch of)

Garnish

toasted bread croutons
Gruyère cheese (grated)

Method

For The Fish

Traditionally scorpion fish, conger eel and gilt head bream were added to bouillabaisse, but at The Millbrook we use fillets of locally-caught fish such as bass, red mullet, gurnard and John Dory, together with some steamed mussels, king prawns and scored squid.

Choose whichever good quality fish is available, and ask your fishmonger to fillet it, but keep the bones and heads for your stock. About 1.3kg of fillet feeds 6 people.

For The Bouillabaisse

Roughly cut all the vegetables into about 1 inch cubes. Sear in oil to a nice golden colour, then add the fish bones. Sweat for 3-4 minutes. Flambé with Pernod and add the white wine. Add the saffron, tomato purée, some salt and pepper and cover with water to about 3-4 inches above the fish bones. Boil the bouillabaisse for 2-3 minutes, then lower the heat and simmer for 2 hours. Mix with a hand blender and pass through a fine sieve. Season to taste.

You have now made the classic Marseillaise fish stew (bouillabaisse) to which any kind of fish can then be added. Simply fry your fillets in a separate frying pan with a little olive oil.

> **Chef's Tip**
>
> Any leftover bouillabaisse sauce (not the fish!) can be frozen and re-heated for another day.

For The Rouille

Combine the garlic, egg yolks, saffron and salt in the bowl of a food processor. Gradually blend in the olive oil, a few drops at a time until the mixture resembles mayonnaise. Once half the oil has been added, stir in the lemon juice and then continue to add the oil to form a thick sauce.

To Serve

Serve the bouillabaisse with the rouille, toasted bread croutons and a little grated Gruyère cheese.

LEMON POSSET WITH LIME SABLE BISCUITS & RASPBERRY SORBET

SERVES 4

A glass of Loupiac, a clean and refreshing white dessert wine, goes well with the more delicate desserts (France)

Ingredients

Lemon Posset

425ml double cream
170g caster sugar
1½ lemons (zest and juice of)

Lime Sable

125g plain flour
75g unsalted butter (softened)
50g caster sugar
1 egg yolk
1 lime (zest of)

Raspberry Sorbet

500g raspberries (fresh or frozen is fine)
60g caster sugar
15ml glucose syrup
1g pectin
125ml water

Garnish

berries

Method

For The Posset

Bring the cream, sugar and lemon zest to the boil and then simmer for 3-4 minutes. Place over an ice bath to cool, strain over the lemon juice then stir together. Set aside for 20 minutes to partially set, and then divide into your chosen glasses. Leave to set in the fridge.

For The Lime Sable

Mix together the butter and sugar until well combined. Fold in the flour and then add the egg yolk and lime zest. Roll into a sausage, wrap in clingfilm and leave in the fridge to chill until it is very firm. Once set, cut into 8 slices, place on greaseproof paper and cook at 180°C for 10 minutes. Sprinkle with caster sugar while hot and then leave to cool.

For The Sorbet

Add all the ingredients except the raspberries to a saucepan and bring to the boil. Cook for about 4-5 minutes until the sugar has dissolved. Crush the raspberries and add to the mixture. Transfer to a freezer-proof container and chill in the freezer until set.

Chef's Tip

You can present this dish in layers. Place a lime sable in a jar, top with some lemon posset and then some raspberries, then another sable biscuit, more lemon posset and some more raspberries, then leave in the fridge to set. Finally, top with the sorbet and some lime zest just before serving.

140
THE OLD COASTGUARD

The Parade, Mousehole, Penzance, Cornwall, TR19 6PR

01736 731 222
www.oldcoastguardhotel.co.uk

The Old Coastguard has been under the auspices of Charles and Edmund Inkin and their EATDRINKSLEEP team since June 2011. It's the most recent addition to a stable which includes The Felin Fach Griffin in Wales and The Gurnard's Head just over the moor in Zennor.

This is a 14-bedroom inn sitting atop the rocks of Mousehole, perhaps the most typical of Cornish fishing villages. Head chef Tom Symons, south west born and trained, prioritises small suppliers from around west Cornwall. A favourite is Bill Johnson who leaves a surprise in a cool box by the kitchen door most mornings, anything from crab or lobster to mackerel or pollock.

The menu, an uncomplicated combination of west Cornwall's finest ingredients, typifies EATDRINKSLEEP's belief in the simple things in life, done well. Mousehole is just three miles along the coast from Newlyn, so naturally seafood forms a good part of the menu, but local game, poultry and meat play their role too and the team is careful to look after non-meat or fish eaters as well.

An award-winning wine list changes to match the seasonal swings in ingredients, with the grape playing an important part of life at The Old Coastguard. And the choice of beers revolves constantly, all sourced from an increasing number of ambitious Cornish brewers.

Relish Restaurant Rewards
See page 003 for details.

The Inkins' company is called EAT**DRINK**SLEEP with good reason. The team brings together the three elements seamlessly. Upstairs are the bedrooms, nearly all looking out over glistening Cornish inland waters, with views to St Michael's Mount and The Lizard.

Ever since the Inkins came to West Penwith in 2006, they have adopted its slower pace of life, providing an opportunity for guests to escape from everyday civilisation. The Old Coastguard is open all year round and lies at the heart of an area teeming with wonderful beaches, historic gardens and the work of renowned artists. Dogs are as welcome as their owners.

GAZPACHO, WHITE CRAB, BASIL

SERVES 4

Fino, La Bota, Equipo Navazos
(Spain)

Ingredients

Gazpacho

750g plum tomatoes (good quality, over ripe)
100g cucumber (peeled, finely sliced)
100g red pepper (finely sliced)
50g fennel (finely sliced)
50g celery (finely sliced)
25g shallots (finely sliced)
2 cloves garlic (finely sliced)
25g white bread (stale)
75ml extra virgin olive oil
5ml sherry vinegar
salt (to taste)
Fino sherry (to taste)
Tabasco (to taste)
1 lemon (juice of)

For The Crab

100g white crabmeat
lemon (squeeze of)
salt

Garnish

basil leaves
extra virgin olive oil

Method

For The Gazpacho (Marinate for at least 2 hours)

Combine all the ingredients in a bowl, season with salt and mix with your hands to form a pulp. Cover and leave to marinate at room temperature for at least 2 hours. Blend in a food processor until smooth and pass through a fine sieve. Season to taste with salt, Tabasco and Fino sherry and place in the fridge until chilled.

For The Crab

Check for shell by running the meat between your fingers. Season with salt and a squeeze of lemon juice.

To Serve

Pour the gazpacho into chilled bowls and place the crabmeat on top, finish with fresh basil leaves and a drizzle of extra virgin olive oil.

> **Chef's Tip**
>
> This soup is for late summer when there is a glut of tomatoes and Cornish crab is at its best.

RAY WING, PICKLED BEETROOT, BRAISED SHALLOTS, COASTLINE GREENS

SERVES 4

🍷 *Saint-Aubin La Fontenotte 2008, Domaine Marc Colin (France)*

Ingredients

Pickled Beetroot

700g beetroot
200ml red wine vinegar
200g caster sugar
200ml water

Braised Shallots

300g round shallots (peeled)
10g butter
100ml chicken stock
2 sprigs fresh thyme

Coastline Greens

200g sea beet
100g rock samphire

Ray Wing And Brown Butter

4 x 250g ray wing portions
light rapeseed oil (for frying)
150g unsalted butter
1 lemon (juice of)
10g capers
salt (to season)

Method

Preheat the oven to 180°C.

For The Pickled Beetroot

Heat the red wine vinegar and sugar in a pan until the sugar has dissolved. Add the water and set aside. Bring the beetroot to the boil in salted water then turn down to a gentle simmer until just cooked. Remove from the pan to cool, then peel and dice into cubes and add to the vinegar. Leave to pickle.

For The Braised Shallots

Season the shallots with a little salt. Melt the butter in a pan, add the shallots and cook for 1 minute until the butter starts to foam. Add the chicken stock, thyme and cover with greaseproof paper. Cook slowly until the shallots are tender and the stock has reduced to a glaze.

For The Ray Wing And Brown Butter

Season the ray with salt. Heat a large non-stick frying pan over a medium heat with the oil. Place the ray wing, thick side down, in the pan and cook for 2 minutes or until the edges colour.

Place the pan into the oven without turning the fish and prepare the coastline greens.

After 4 minutes, turn the fish and add the butter. Cook for a further minute on the hob and then remove from the pan. Continue to cook the butter until it turns to a nut brown and then add the lemon juice to stop the cooking. Take care as it may spit.

For The Coastline Greens

Remove any woody stalks from the greens. Add the sea beet to a hot pan with a pinch of salt and a little water and allow to wilt. Add the samphire and cook for a further 30 seconds.

To Serve

Stir the brown butter, pickled beetroot, braised shallots and capers together. Add salt and extra lemon to taste. Place the ray wings on warmed plates and share out the coastline greens. Spoon over the warm beetroot and braised shallot sauce.

> **Chef's Tip**
>
> For a healthier version of this dish, omit the butter in the sauce and use quality cold pressed rapeseed oil to make a warm dressing.

BLACKBERRY JELLY, FENNEL PANNA COTTA, MERINGUE

SERVES 4

 Tarquin's Handcrafted Cornish Pastis, Southwestern Distillery (England)

Ingredients

Blackberry Jelly

500g blackberries
100ml water
75g sugar
2 star anise
10ml lemon juice
1½ gelatine leaves (soaked in water)
40ml Cornish pastis

Fennel Panna Cotta

300ml double cream
75ml milk
75g caster sugar
½ lemon (zest of)
150g fennel (finely sliced)
1 star anise
1½ gelatine leaves (soaked in water)

Blackberry Ice Cream

600g blackberries
½ lemon (juice of)
4 free-range egg yolks
120g caster sugar
250ml full-fat milk
250ml double cream

Italian Meringue

3 egg whites
350g caster sugar
50ml water
1 tsp glucose

Garnish

blackberries (halved)

Chef's Tip

If sugar crystals begin to form when making the syrup for the Italian meringue, pass a clean pastry brush around the inside edge of the pan to remove them.

Method

For The Blackberry Jelly

Heat the first 5 ingredients in a saucepan and simmer for 5 minutes. Pour through a muslin lined sieve and drain. Do not press the pulp as this will make the jelly cloudy.

Measure 400ml of the collected blackberry liquid into a clean pan and cook slowly until just warm. Whisk in the gelatine until the lumps dissolve. Remove from the heat, allow to cool and add the pastis. Pour into 4 glasses and chill in the fridge.

For The Fennel Panna Cotta

Place all the ingredients, except the gelatine, into a pan. Gently bring to the boil, then remove from the heat and cover. Allow to infuse for 30 minutes and then pass through a fine sieve. Heat the liquid in a clean pan until just warm. Whisk in the gelatine until any lumps are dissolved and allow to cool. Pour the fennel cream onto the set blackberry jelly and place back in the fridge to set.

For The Blackberry Ice Cream

Purée the blackberries and half of the lemon juice in a blender, then pass through a sieve into a pan. Place over a low heat and reduce by half. Measure 250ml and set aside.

Whisk the egg yolks with 60g of the caster sugar in a large bowl until thick and creamy.

Place the remaining ingredients and blackberry purée in a pan and bring to the boil. Pour the mixture into the egg yolks and stir well. Return all to the pan and cook over a very low heat, stirring constantly with a spatula until it coats the back of a spoon (79-81ºC). Remove from the heat, strain, taste and add more lemon if desired. Cover and cool. Churn in an ice cream machine, or see page 231.

For The Italian Meringue

Place the egg whites in a mixer and whisk until they have doubled in size. Meanwhile, put the remaining ingredients in a pan and cook until the liquid reaches 121ºC (do not overheat the sugar mixture or leave unattended).

Slowly pour the sugar syrup onto the egg whites. Continue to whisk the meringue mixture for 10-15 minutes until thick, glossy and cold. Transfer to a piping bag and store in the fridge.

To Serve

Pipe the meringue on top of the panna cotta and brown the edges with a cook's blowtorch. Serve with the ice cream and halved blackberries.

150
THE OLIVE TREE RESTAURANT

The Queensberry Hotel, 4-7 Russel Street, Bath, BA1 2QF

01225 447 928
www.olivetreebath.co.uk

The Olive Tree Restaurant will be celebrating its 25th birthday in 2014 and has long been on the foodie radar in the south west. The restaurant is known for consistently serving excellent food to Bathonians and visitors to the beautiful city alike.

When I had the opportunity to join the team early in 2013, I jumped at the chance. I saw this as an opportunity to build on The Olive Tree's reputation, to push the standards of food higher than ever before and to help the restaurant achieve even greater acclaim.

In my career to date I have had the privilege of working alongside some of those whom I consider to be the most talented and inspirational chefs in the UK, including Michael Caines, Heston Blumenthal and Adam Simmonds. From them I have learnt the classical and modern techniques of food preparation, and perhaps most importantly, their work ethic, ethos towards food and the absolute commitment to never compromise standards. At The Olive Tree I am now able to bring all that into my own style of modern British cuisine, offering beautifully balanced dishes which deliver on flavour and delight our guests.

Bath is such a fantastic city, and being one of the most visited in the UK, I am lucky to have the opportunity to cook for people from all over the world. It is extremely important to me to showcase the fantastic produce available to us in this region and to reflect seasonality throughout the menu. Relationships are so important in this business, for example, knowing I can rely on my local farmer to grow a specific crop of vegetables for a garnish and to harvest them at the optimum point is essential to the success of the final dish.
Head Chef, Chris Cleghorn

Relish Restaurant Rewards
See page 003 for details.

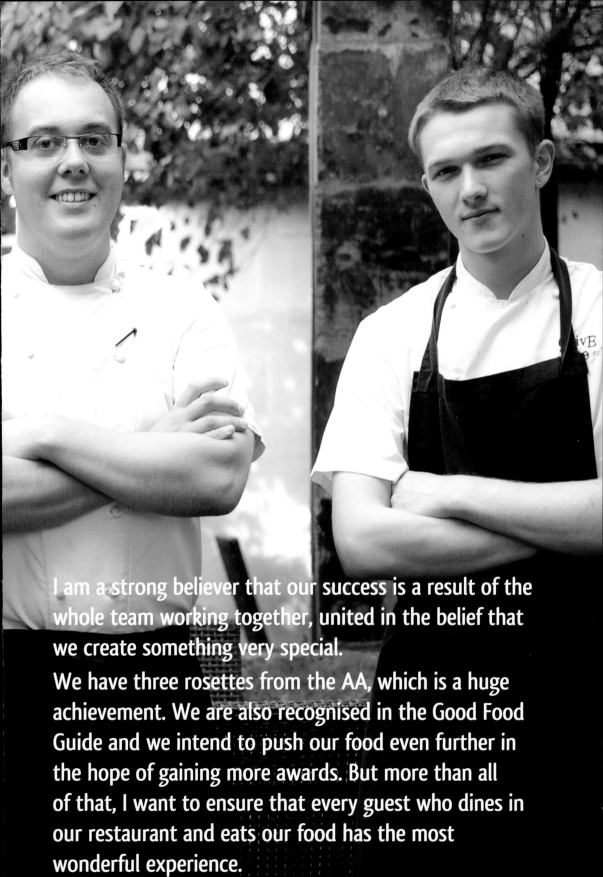

I am a strong believer that our success is a result of the whole team working together, united in the belief that we create something very special.

We have three rosettes from the AA, which is a huge achievement. We are also recognised in the Good Food Guide and we intend to push our food even further in the hope of gaining more awards. But more than all of that, I want to ensure that every guest who dines in our restaurant and eats our food has the most wonderful experience.

CURED & CHARRED MACKEREL, CUCUMBER, AVOCADO & LIME

SERVES 8

 Vernaccia di San Gimignano, Panizzi, Tuscany, 2010 (Italy)

Ingredients

4 whole fresh mackerel

Salad

1 cucumber (halved lengthways)
1 avocado
2 limes
borage (flowers and leaves)
fresh dill
1 lime (juice of)

Pickling Liquor

650ml water
75ml white wine vinegar
5g coriander seeds (toasted)
30g white peppercorns
10g salt
10g sugar
2 bay leaves
5 cloves garlic (crushed)

Mackerel Cure

25g salt
25g sugar
ground white pepper (pinch of)
1 lime (zest of)
5g coriander seeds (toasted and crushed)
10g fresh dill (chopped)

Method

For The Pickling Liquor (Prepare the day before)

Toast the coriander seeds and place with the rest of the ingredients in a pan. Bring to the boil, remove from the heat, cover with clingfilm and infuse for 30 minutes. Strain off the liquor and keep chilled until required.

For The Cucumber Strips And Balls

Use a small parisienne scoop to ball out half of the cucumber. Cut the other half of the cucumber into thin slices, approximately 1mm thick and 12cm long. Place the cucumber in a container with the pickling liquor for at least 24 hours.

For The Mackerel And Cure

Toast the coriander seeds in a pan and then lightly crush. Mix with the salt, sugar, lime zest, pepper and dill.

Fillet the mackerel and remove the bones and blood line from the middle of the fillets. Trim the fillets so that they are even in size, approximately 12cm in length.

Cover a flat tray in clingfilm and spread the cure evenly over the tray. Place the fillets flesh side down on the cure, taking care not to get any onto the skin of the mackerel as this will harden it. Leave the fillets to cure for 90 minutes in a refrigerator. Remove from the fridge and wash off the cure, place on a cloth and keep in the fridge until ready to use.

To Serve

Use a small parisienne scoop to ball out the avocado. Mix the sliced pickled cucumber, pickled cucumber balls and the avocado in a bowl with the chopped dill and the lime juice.

Place one slice of pickled cucumber onto the middle of each plate. Arrange 5 pickled cucumber balls in 2 lines below the sliced cucumber. Place some small avocado balls between the cucumber balls. Place 3 lime segments in between. Garnish with borage leaves and flowers. Finally, take a fillet of mackerel. Using a blow torch, sear the skin of the fish until the skin crisps and is golden in colour. Flip the fish over, dress with a little lime juice and sea salt. Place onto the sliced cucumber skin-side up.

VEAL WITH SHALLOT PUREE, BOULANGERE POTATO, CREAMED CABBAGE & VEAL JUS

SERVES 8

 *Charles Schleret Pinot Noir, Alsace, 2007
(France)*

Ingredients

Loin Of Veal

8 x 100g veal loin (ask your butcher to trim)
1 tbsp olive oil
8 sprigs thyme
1 onion (finely sliced in 2mm rings)

Boulangère Potato

8 large potatoes (peeled and washed)
1 large onion (very finely sliced)
butter (knob of, melted)
chicken stock (to cover)
salt and pepper

Creamed Cabbage

2 large Savoy cabbages
350ml double cream
60g garlic (crushed)

Roasted Shallots

8 banana shallots (peeled and halved lengthways)
90ml port
60g butter
1 sprig thyme (leaves picked)

Shallot Purée

1½kg banana shallots (thinly sliced)
110g butter

Chef's Tip

A *mandolin*, available from any good kitchen shop, is a valuable tool for slicing vegetables very thinly.

Method

For The Veal

Preheat the oven to 180°C. Heat a small amount of oil in a heavy-bottomed frying pan and seal the outside of the loin on all sides. Place the thyme in the pan with the onion and roast the veal in the oven for 10 minutes or until the centre of the meat reaches 58°C. This will be pink on the inside, roast for longer if you prefer the meat well cooked. Remove the veal from the pan and rest for 5 minutes. Slice each loin into 4 even slices and retain the veal *jus*.

For The Veal Jus

Add 100ml of water to the veal cooking *jus*. Bring to the boil and pass through a sieve. Keep warm.

For The Potatoes

Preheat the oven to 180°C. Sweat the onions in melted butter until soft and opaque. Slice the potatoes into thin slices, approximately 1mm thick. Make a layer of sliced potato in a deep baking tray, then cover with a layer of onion and season with salt and pepper. Continue building until you have 8 layers. Cover with chicken stock. Place greaseproof paper over the potatoes and place a baking dish on top of the greaseproof paper to press down the boulangère. Bake in the oven for 2 hours. Remove from the oven and check that the potato is cooked, then cool. When cold, remove from the container and cut into 8 equal squares.

For The Cabbage

Discard the outer leaves of cabbage. Wash then slice the rest into thin strips. *Blanch* in hot salted water. Reduce the cream by two thirds in a large pan with the crushed garlic until the cream becomes very thick. Add the garlic cream to the *blanched* cabbage, stir and season.

For The Roasted Shallots

Place the shallots sliced side down in a heavy frying pan and cook until golden brown. Add the butter to the pan and turn the shallots. Add the port and thyme, transfer to the oven (still at 180°C) and roast for 8-10 minutes until soft.

For The Shallot Purée

Melt 60g of the butter in a pan and, when foaming, add the shallots and season. Cook out slowly with no colour until completely soft and no moisture remains in the pan. Blend until smooth. Check the seasoning and add the rest of the butter.

To Serve

Heat a heavy frying pan with a little oil and seal both sides of the cooled boulangère potato squares. Place in a hot oven, 200°C, for 10 minutes to heat through. Place a square of potato on the side of each plate. Swipe some of the warm shallot purée across the middle of the plate with a spoon. Place a spoonful of the cabbage next to the purée, the sliced veal on top of the cabbage and the roasted shallots on top of the veal. Finish with a spoonful of veal *jus* around the cabbage.

BLUEBERRY CHEESECAKE WITH BLUEBERRY SORBET

SERVES 8

*Rudera Noble Late Harvest Chenin Blanc,
Stellenbosch (South Africa)*

Ingredients

Stock Syrup

350g sugar
350g water

Blueberry Purée

250g blueberries
250ml stock syrup

Cheesecake Base

250g ground almonds
250g sugar
250g unsalted butter
250g plain flour
80g honey
100g *clarified* butter

Cheesecake

500g cream cheese
350ml natural yoghurt
150ml double cream
1 orange, 1 lemon (zest of)
1 vanilla pod (split lengthways, seeds scraped out)
180g icing sugar
3½ leaves gold leaf gelatine (soaked in water)

Blueberry Sorbet

500g blueberry purée
blueberry liqueur (to taste)
50ml lemon juice
26g sorbet stabiliser (available online)
300ml stock syrup

Blueberry Jelly

500g blueberry purée
100ml stock syrup
3 leaves gold leaf gelatine (soaked in water)
50g lemon juice

Garnish

blueberries, candied orange peel

8cm x 4cm moulds

Method

For The Stock Syrup
Heat the sugar in the water until dissolved. Set aside to use in the purée, sorbet and jelly.

For The Blueberry Purée
Liquidise the blueberries and stock syrup together. Pass through a sieve and reserve until needed.

For The Cheesecake Base
Blend all the base ingredients together in a mixer, excluding the *clarified* butter, until it forms a crumb texture. Spread the mixture out on a metal baking sheet and cook at 180°C until evenly golden. Keep moving the crumb around the tray to gain an even bake.

Pour the *clarified* butter over the crumb and combine the ingredients. Roll out the crumb between 2 pieces of greaseproof paper until 3mm thick. Set in the fridge for 10 minutes and then stamp your moulds into the crumb.

For The Cheesecake
Cream the yoghurt and cream cheese together in a large mixing bowl. Bring the cream, orange zest, lemon zest, icing sugar, vanilla pod and seeds to a simmer in a heavy-bottomed pan. Add the soaked gelatine, then pass the mixture through a fine sieve. Add to the creamed yoghurt and cream cheese. Check the taste of the mixture and add more sugar according to preference. With the crumb already in the base of the moulds, fill to the top and scrape flat with a palette knife. Refrigerate and leave to set for at least 3 hours.

For The Sorbet
Blend the ingredients together using a liquidiser. Pass through a fine sieve, churn in an ice cream machine, or see page 231.

For The Jelly
Reduce the blueberry purée by half in a heavy-bottomed metal pan over a medium heat. When the soaked gelatine is soft, add to the reduced blueberry purée. Add the stock syrup and lemon juice and mix. Pass through a fine sieve into a storage container. When the jelly is cool, but not set, pour a small amount onto the set cheesecake. With a small palette knife, spread the jelly evenly over the top of the mould to create a layer of jelly approximately 2mm thick.

To Serve
Remove the cheesecake from the mould and place on a serving plate. Dress the cheesecake with fresh blueberries and candied orange peel. Serve with the blueberry sorbet and blueberry purée.

Chef's Tip
Use a kitchen blow torch to very slightly warm the sides of the moulds to release the cheesecake.

160
THE QUEENS ARMS

Corton Denham, Sherborne, Somerset, DT9 4LR

01963 220 317
www.thequeensarms.com

The Queens Arms in Corton Denham is a family-run, 18th Century country inn, nestled in the hills that form the Dorset and Somerset border. It is situated in undulating countryside, two miles from medieval Sherborne with its stunning castles and Abbey.

The Queens is the best in the region, having won the Taste of Somerset Best Pub Award, Best National Freehouse Award, an AA rosette and the Somerset CAMRA Cider Pub of the Year.

It is run by husband, wife and son team, Gordon, Jeanette and Kyle Reid, who source their fruit, vegetables and most of their meat from the local village. They have their own established farm producing the finest free range products including their own eggs and pork.

"Our menus are designed to reflect the best seasonally available food that this famous agricultural area has to offer," says Jeanette. Whether you want to try the award-winning restaurant menu, or classic pub menu, The Queens will provide wholesome, creative and well prepared real food.

Visitors looking for a romantic getaway or a quiet escape can also enjoy The Queens quintessentially English hospitality.

Its eight luxury rooms, with state of the art bathrooms, have every detail covered, including L'Occitane bathroom products, soft dressing gowns and slippers, a range of herbal teas and 100% Egyptian cotton bed linen, to delight those looking for something special.

Relish Restaurant Rewards
See page 003 for details.

A team of chefs work under team leaders Arnie Fernandes and Ben Abercombie, delivering a range of culinary dishes. The creative team pair the likes of pork and toffee apple and create carrot cakes that look like a forest floor.

The team makes everything fresh including ice cream, bread and preserves: they believe making simple dishes well is the key to success. The focus for The Queens Arms has always been on sustainability and locally-sourced produce.

PRAWN TORTELLINI, TEMPURA CRAB CLAW, MUSHROOM & BROWN SHRIMP BUTTER

SERVES 4

 Viognier, Podere di Montelupa VDT Ascheri, Piemonte (Italy)

Ingredients

Pasta
250g pasta flour
2 eggs
3 egg yolks
salt (pinch of)

Filling
6 large prawns (peeled)
½ lemon (juice and zest of)
1 tsp dill
salt (to taste)

Crab Claws
4 crab claws (cleaned)
100g self-raising flour
150g cornflour
200ml lemonade
300ml cooking oil

Mushroom And Brown Shrimp Butter
100g butter
250g girolle mushrooms
100g brown shrimp
1 lemon (juice of)

Method

For The Prawn Filling
Blend all the ingredients into a paste consistency and set aside.

For The Tortellini
Sieve the pasta flour into a bowl and add the eggs, egg yolks and salt. Combine to a dough, wrap with clingfilm and chill in the fridge for 20 minutes. Pass through a pasta machine to thickness setting 2 and place on a lightly floured surface. Cut into discs of 80mm diameter.

Take a teaspoon of the prawn filling and place in the centre of a disc. Fold into a half moon shape, hold the pasta between your little and ring finger and pinch the ends together to make tortellini shapes.

For The Crab Claw
Ask your fishmonger to prepare and clean 4 crab claws. Mix both flours in a large mixing bowl with the lemonade and salt. Whisk together to make a batter and set aside.

> **Chef's Tip**
> Roll out the pasta using semolina flour to prevent it from sticking to your worktop.

For The Mushroom And Brown Shrimp Butter
Melt half the butter into a pan, add the girolles and cook for 3 minutes until soft. Add the brown shrimp, the remaining butter and the lemon juice. Set aside until required.

To Serve
Cook the tortellini for 3-4 minutes in a pan of boiling water. Heat the cooking oil in a separate pan on a low heat, dip the crab claw into the batter and fry in the oil for 3 minutes.

Place the tortellini onto your dish, pour over the mushroom and shrimp butter and serve the crab claw on top.

DUO OF PORK - SLOW ROAST BELLY & SALTIMBOCCA TENDERLOIN, FONDANT POTATO, CELERIAC PUREE, CIDER & THYME JUS

SERVES 4

 The FMC Chenin, Ken Forrester (South Africa)

Ingredients

Pork Belly

500g best end pork belly (seasoned)
1 bulb garlic
1 carrot, 1 medium onion (cut into rough chunks)
285ml sweet cider, 570ml pint water
4 sprigs thyme
salt and pepper (to season)

Saltimbocca Tenderloin

1 pork tenderloin (cleaned and trimmed)
4 slices Parma ham
8 leaves sage
salt and pepper (to season)

Confit Potato

4 good sized red rooster potatoes (peeled and trimmed at both ends)
2 sprigs rosemary, ½ bulb garlic
800ml vegetable oil
400ml goose or duck fat

Celeriac Purée

300g celeriac
500ml water, 75g butter
salt and pepper (to season)

Cider Jus

braising liquor (from the pork belly)
100ml sweet cider, 250ml double cream
1 tbsp Dijon mustard

Caramelised Apples

4 baby or small apples
50g sugar, 10ml water, lemon juice (squeeze of)

Garnish

4 heritage carrots, micro herbs

Method

For The Pork Belly
Preheat the oven to 150ºC. Place all the ingredients into a deep oven tray, placing the seasoned pork belly, skin side up, on top. Cover with parchment paper to stop it sticking and wrap airtight in foil. Place in the oven for 2½ hours or until tender. Remove the tray, press with a weight and chill. Cut into 4½cm squares and set aside. When ready to serve, crisp the belly under a grill until it is a nutty, golden brown. Keep the stock from the pork belly for the sauce.

For The Saltimbocca Tenderloin
Lightly season the tenderloin and cut into 4 equal pieces. Roll a piece of tenderloin and 2 sage leaves in each slice of Parma ham. Set aside.

For The Confit Potato
Heat the oil and fat, rosemary and garlic in a large pan. Add the potatoes, ensuring that they are completely covered in oil. Cook on a low heat for 45-60 minutes. Strain and season.

For The Celeriac Purée
Put the celeriac, water, salt and pepper in a saucepan and cook until tender. Pour into a sieve and leave for 5 minutes to drain. Using a hand blender, roughly blend the celeriac to a course consistency. Add a knob of butter to the purée to taste.

For The Caramelised Apples
Heat the sugar and water in a pan to form a caramel. Add a splash of lemon juice to stop it from crystallising. Set aside to cool slightly, then roll the apples in the caramel.

For The Cider Jus
Pour the braising stock from the pork belly into a *chinois*. Press down with a ladle so you get all the juices from the vegetables. Bring the cider to the boil in a saucepan, burning off all the alcohol. Add the stock and reduce by half. Add the double cream and Dijon mustard, then adjust with seasoning.

To Serve
Preheat the oven to 150ºC. Line an oven tray with greaseproof paper then sprinkle with a little cooking oil. Arrange your tenderloins and confit potatoes on the tray and cook in the oven for 6 minutes. Take out the tenderloins and leave to rest for a further 4 minutes.

Smear the purée onto a plate using a spoon. Arrange the pork belly, tenderloin, potatoes and vegetables as pictured and drizzle with *jus*. Garnish with a caramelised apple, a sprinkle of micro herbs and serve with steamed heritage carrots.

FOREST FLOOR DECONSTRUCTED CARROT & WALNUT CAKE WITH SALTED CARAMEL & PISTACHIO ICE CREAM, CANDIED CARROTS

SERVES 4

🍷 *Botrytised Viognier, Trinity Hill, Hawkes Bay (New Zealand)*

Ingredients

Carrot Cake
325ml vegetable oil
425g soft brown sugar
300g self-raising flour (sieved)
1 tsp table salt
10g cinnamon
4 eggs
110g walnuts (toasted, roughly chopped)
375g carrots (finely grated)

Soil
750g caster sugar, water (splash of)
100g dark chocolate (broken into pieces)

Ice Cream
570ml full-fat milk, 570ml double cream
12 egg yolks
50g sugar
400g pistachio nuts (blitzed until chunky)

Caramel
450g sugar, 450ml water
lemon juice (squeeze of), salt (pinch of)

Caramel Tunnel
50g sugar, 100ml water, 1 lemon (juice of)

Butter Icing
140g butter (soft, at room temperature)
280g icing sugar, 2 tbsp double cream

Candied Carrots
8 Chantilly carrots (peeled and washed)
sweetened water (to cover)
1 orange (juice of)

Garnish
mint leaves, micro basil
winter berries (dusted with icing sugar)
2 vanilla pods (split), 8 small chocolate buttons

25cm springform cake tin (oiled and lined)

Method

For The Carrot Cake
Preheat the oven to 200°C. Cream together the oil and sugar in a mixing bowl, then add the flour, salt and cinnamon. Gently stir in the eggs, then fold in the walnuts and carrots. Turn into the prepared cake tin. Turn the oven down to 160°C and bake for 30 minutes.

For The Soil
Dissolve the sugar and water over a low heat. Reduce down on a high temperature until golden. Add the broken up chocolate then stir quickly together. Remove from the heat and leave to cool.

For The Salted Caramel And Pistachio Ice Cream
Pour the milk and cream into a pan and bring to the boil. Take care not to let it boil over. Put the 450g sugar and 450ml water and salt into another pan, adding a squeeze of lemon juice, stir once and place on a medium heat. Do not stir the caramel mixture. When it turns a golden brown colour, take off the heat and pour directly into the boiling milk and cream. Whisk the caramel in thoroughly and reduce the heat to low.

Whisk the eggs and sugar in a bowl. Bring the caramel back to the boil and pour half of it into the egg mixture. Whisk together and pour back into the pan. Stir slowly over a low heat with a spatula. Once it thickens, strain through a sieve and place in the fridge to cool. When cool, churn in an ice cream machine, or see page 231.

For The Butter Icing
Beat the butter in a large bowl until smooth and creamy. Add the sugar slowly, keep beating the mixture then add the cream and beat again until the icing is smooth. Lightly drag the tip of a hot teaspoon through a spoonful of icing to make a flower, as shown.

For The Candied Carrots
Place the carrots in a pan with the orange juice and top up with sweetened water to cover. Cook until tender. Leave to cool.

For The Caramel Tunnel
Dissolve the sugar in water over a high heat then bring to the boil, reduce until golden. Leave to cool slightly, then spin the caramel over a wooden spoon and bundle together to form a tunnel.

To Serve
Make the mouse using a hot ice cream scoop to form the body. Add 2 small chocolate buttons for eyes and half a vanilla pod for the tail. Arrange the other elements as pictured.

170
THE SALTY MONK

Church Street, Sidford, Sidmouth, Devon, EX10 9QP

01395 513 174
www.saltymonk.co.uk

Andy and Annette Witheridge have a simple philosophy on food. They serve honest dishes that are big on flavour and unfussy in style. Supremely consistent, their east Devon restaurant has been awarded two AA rosettes for nine consecutive years.

The Salty Monk is also a uniquely charming hotel, which has wowed customers for more than a dozen years. It has earned a five star gold rating with Visit England and the AA since its inception. And the industrious and creative couple's achievements do not end there. In recent years, they have been both the winner and the runner-up of the Best Bed and Breakfast in the UK.

Andy and Annette bought The Salty Monk just before the millennium, when the venue was just a shell. Since then, they've transformed it into one of the south west's most sought-after locations. Stunning artworks adorn the walls of their cool, contemporary bar while sumptuous bouquets fill the dining room.

The couple has taken buying local to a new level. "If somebody's good at something and they're honest about it, we'll work with them," says Andy. "But we don't buy from big suppliers.

We don't need to. We can get everything we need from the south west. Our ingredients, our drinks, our art and our tableware are all bought from small, sustainable artisan businesses."

Their Michelin-rated venue features in the Good Food Guide and they make everything on the premises, from breads and stocks to pastas, sauces and sausages. They even cure their own bacon.

"We have people who grow and breed things for us," says Andy. "That helps us to control the quality and deliver the best possible flavours time after time after time."

Relish Restaurant Rewards
See page 003 for details.

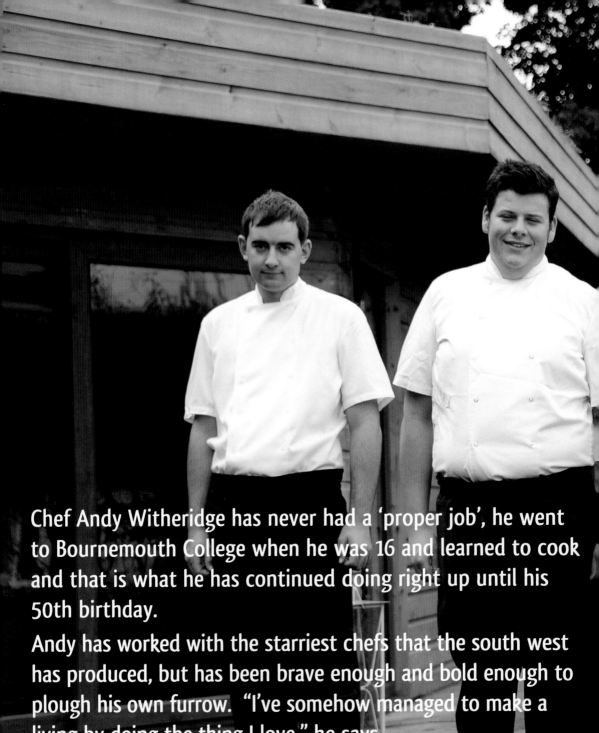

Chef Andy Witheridge has never had a 'proper job', he went to Bournemouth College when he was 16 and learned to cook and that is what he has continued doing right up until his 50th birthday.

Andy has worked with the starriest chefs that the south west has produced, but has been brave enough and bold enough to plough his own furrow. "I've somehow managed to make a living by doing the thing I love," he says.

The Salty Monk is a tribute to Andy and wife Annette's dedication, craft and guile. It celebrates artisanship and artistry, with a focus on the best of local food, artwork and design.

FISH TERRINE WITH A LOBSTER FOAM

SERVES 8

*Chenin Blanc Touraine 2011, Domaine Pascal
Pibaleau (France)*

Ingredients

8 large scallops (with roe)
200g fresh salmon
1 pack sushi nori

Scallop And Salmon Mousse

8 scallop roes
50g fresh salmon
10g sea salt
3 medium egg whites
75ml whipping cream

Sole Mousse

250g sole fillets
10g sea salt
8 egg whites
150ml whipping cream

Lobster Foam

3 cubes lobster glaze (see tip)
50ml whipping cream
50ml full-fat milk
50g butter (cold, cubed)

Method

For The Mousses

Semi-freeze the fish until just icing. To make the sole mousse, blitz the fish and salt in a food processor for 2-3 minutes until stringy, slowly add the egg whites then the cream. It is important to keep the mixture ice cold, returning it to the freezer before serving if necessary. For best results, pass through a sieve. To make the salmon and scallop mousse, start by blitzing the salmon and the roe in a food processor, then repeat the above process.

For The Terrine

First line your terrine mould with clingfilm, then line with sushi nori (no need to dampen). Pipe a line of salmon mousse along another sheet of nori the same length as your mould, roll into a cylinder. Repeat so you have 4 in total. Layer the rest of the mousse in the lined terrine mould along with the strips of salmon fillet and the nori rolls. Fold in the nori over the top of the mousse, cover with the clingfilm and put a lid on. Bake in a water bath, slowly, until it reaches 69°C.

To Serve

Sear the scallops in a hot pan, then set aside. *Deglaze* the pan with the lobster glaze, add the milk and cream, then bring to the boil. Whizz with an electric wand, adding the cold butter cubes. Slice the terrine, place on a warm plate and garnish with a seared scallop. Spoon over some of the lobster foam and serve immediately.

> **Chef's Tip**
>
> When poaching a lobster, save the cooking liquor, add the crushed shells, simmer for 1 hour and strain. Return to a clean pan, reduce to a glaze and freeze in ice cube trays.

GRIDDLED SIRLOIN STEAK WITH SHIN FILLED WILD GARLIC RAVIOLI

SERVES 6-8

 Urban Uco Malbec, Mendoza, 2012
(Argentina)

Ingredients

200g sirloin steak (per person, larder trimmed)

Wild Garlic Pasta

500g strong 00 flour
8 egg yolks
2 whole eggs
10g salt
100g wild garlic leaves

Sauce

1kg bones (veal or beef)
1 large onion (roughly chopped)
1 large carrot (roughly chopped)
½ stick celery (roughly chopped)
1 bottle red wine

Ravioli Filling

500g beef shin (cooked)
horseradish sauce (to taste)
mustard (to taste)

seasonal vegetables (optional)

Method

For The Sauce (Prepare the day before)

Roast the trimmed shin and bones with the vegetables in a deep roasting dish until golden. Cover in red wine and water and slow cook at 85°C for 8 hours. Ladle any fat off the top during the cooking, keeping the sauce crystal clear. Strain, retaining all of the vegetables, and chill overnight. Very slowly reduce the stock by three quarters, skimming off any impurities.

For The Wild Garlic Pasta

Blend the garlic leaves, flour and salt as much as possible, aiming for green flour! (See tip). Leave the flour to cool if it has heated with friction. Knead in the eggs to form a tight, crumbly dough. Chill for 1 hour.

> **Chef's Tip**
>
> If you have a Thermomix, you can mill your green flour in 30 seconds at speed 10.

For The Ravioli Filling (Prepare the day before)

Dice the cooked shin, lightly crush the vegetables from the stock and mix together, adding horseradish and mustard to taste. Aim for plenty of flavour as the pasta will absorb the taste when cooked.

To Make The Ravioli

Halve your pasta dough and, using a pasta machine, roll out into 2 separate sheets on the thinnest setting. Wash lightly with some beaten egg. Make small piles of the shin filling on one of the sheets, each about 1 tablespoon, ensuring each spoonful of filling is approximately 6cm away from the next. Lay the second sheet over the top, pressing down to remove all the air. Cut out into circles around each mound of filling, leaving a 1cm edge of pasta all the way around. Re-roll the trimmings into tagliatelle. Cover the ravioli with a clean cloth and refrigerate until needed.

To Serve

Season the steaks well, then panfry or griddle to your taste. Cover with foil and rest in a warm place for 10 minutes.

Add 1 tablespoon of olive oil to a pan of salted boiling water and cook the ravioli for 4 minutes. In a separate pan, cook the tagliatelle for 2 minutes.

Place a nest of tagliatelle on the plate, place the steak then garnish with ravioli and the warmed reduced shin sauce.

BAKED ALASKA
A RETURN TO THE 70s

SERVES 6-8

🍷 *Paul Cluver Noble Late Harvest Riesling 2011, Elgin (South Africa)*

Ingredients

Italian Meringue

5 medium egg whites
200g caster sugar

Ice Cream

5 egg yolks
125g caster sugar
500ml whipping cream
125ml milk
125ml natural Greek yoghurt
50ml runny honey

Génoise Sponge Base

4 medium eggs
125g caster sugar
125g plain flour

Garnish

Greek yoghurt
cinder toffee
honeycomb

30cm Swiss roll tin

Method

For The Ice Cream

Whisk the egg yolks and sugar until white. Boil the cream and milk and pour onto the egg mixture, whisking carefully. Return the mixture to the heat and cook slowly until 83°C, or until it coats the back of a wooden spoon. Pour the custard mix into the honey and yoghurt and stir well. Chill for 2 hours then churn in an ice cream machine, or see page 231.

> **Chef's Tip**
>
> Make your ice cream a day or two before you intend to serve this dessert. Alternatively, you can buy any flavour ice cream you fancy and change with the seasons if you don't have an ice cream machine.

For The Génoise Sponge

Whisk the whole eggs and sugar until foamy and pale. A trail will be left when picking up the whisk. Fold in the flour by hand, taking care not to knock out any air. Pour into a greased, 30cm Swiss roll tin and cook at 150°C for 20-25 minutes. Cool, then using a 7cm circular cutter, cut individual bases. Top with a ball of the ice cream and freeze.

For The Italian Meringue

Put the sugar into a spotlessly clean stainless steel pan. Add just enough water to dissolve the sugar and bring to the boil rapidly, until the sugar reaches soft ball stage (113°C.) Remove from the heat and place the bottom of the pan into cold water to remove surplus heat. Whisk the egg whites until they form soft peaks, then pour into the hot sugar, slowly, whilst whisking vigorously. Keep whisking until the mixture is cool, glossy and stiff. Pipe over the cake and ice cream carefully, leaving no holes. Re-freeze the Alaskas until required.

To Serve

Preheat the oven to 175°C and bake for 7 minutes or until lightly golden. Garnish the plates with a spoon of Greek yoghurt, cinder toffee, honeycomb and finally, the baked Alaska. Serve immediately.

180
SAMPHIRE

36 Arwenack Street, Falmouth, Cornwall, TR11 3JF

01326 210 759
www.samphire-falmouth.co.uk

Clean-tasting, simple food that is fresh and packed with flavour is the order of the day at Samphire Restaurant in Falmouth. Chef-patron Dave Trewin adds a unique twist to local ingredients, embracing techniques that extract the maximum flavour from exceptional ingredients.

Rabbit, for instance, might be served with a tandoori ballotine and onion bhaji, while scallops may be pan fried and served with belly pork and cauliflower purée.

Samphire's position, within walking distance of the sea front, means fish features heavily. "We have exceptional contacts with the guys on the day boats," says Dave. "They make sure we get the very best fish and shellfish that they catch. It's a privileged position to be in."

Samphire's honest approach to fresh food, made with local ingredients, has been rewarded with a listing in the Michelin guide. "We were thrilled to be included, but we look at that as just being a start."

Dave and his partner, Emily, are still in their twenties and are among the youngest restaurateurs in the south west. They bring style and panache to their bistro, which is located in one of Cornwall's busiest streets.

Emily adds: "We aim for quality and consistency and we want every customer to leave feeling that they've had a great meal in a welcoming environment."

Relish Restaurant Rewards
See page 003 for details.

Specials

Wine:
Cornish camel valley pinot
noir rosé by the glass £7.65

Starters:
Crab & fennel salad, orange
crème fraîche dressing £7.45

Mains:
Local pollock fillet, crushed
potato, bacon & spinach sorrel
cream sauce £15.95

Dessert:
Honeycomb cheesecake,
chocolate coated, honeycomb,
toffee sauce & fresh strawberries
£5.95

The list of suppliers at Falmouth's Samphire restaurant reads like a 'who's who' of great Cornish producers. "We're proud of our association with the best providers of seasonal food and drink," says chef Dave Trewin. Using produce from Cornish sea salt to Lizard Leaves, from Rodda's clotted cream to Duchy Game, from Camel Valley and Skinners Brewery to Wicketts pork and poultry and Matthew Stevens & Son, Samphire places great value in provenance, quality and seasonality. "We're in an area of remarkable food. We bring fantastic ingredients to the plate and show them every respect."

SLOW COOKED BELLY PORK, BBQ SAUCE & POLENTA CHIPS

SERVES 4

🍷 *ONA Pinot Noir*
(Chile)

Ingredients

Belly Pork

600g belly pork (cooked, cut into 4 equal portions)
pea shoots (to garnish)

BBQ Sauce

1 medium onion (peeled and chopped)
10 cloves garlic (peeled)
2 fresh red chillies
10 sprigs fresh thyme (leaves picked)
10 sprigs fresh rosemary (leaves picked)
1 handful fresh coriander
10 bay leaves
1 tsp cumin seeds, 1 tbsp fennel seeds
2 star anise
3 tbsp smoked paprika
6 cloves
2 oranges (juice and zest of)
200g dark soft brown sugar
4 tbsp balsamic vinegar
200ml tomato ketchup
2 tbsp Worcestershire sauce
2 tsp English mustard
250ml apple juice
sea salt and black pepper (to season)

Beetroot Slaw

1 red onion (peeled)
1 large beetroot (peeled)
200g red cabbage
100g mayonnaise
½ lemon (juice and zest of)
sea salt and black pepper (to season)

Polenta Chips

300ml chicken stock
150g polenta, butter (knob of)
70g Parmesan cheese (grated)
few sprigs thyme (picked)
vegetable oil (to deep fry)
sea salt and black pepper (to season)

Method

For The BBQ Sauce

Blend the onion, garlic and chillies in a food processor until you've got a really fine paste. Gently fry the paste on a low heat in some olive oil for roughly 5 minutes. Now add all the herbs and spices to the food processor with the orange zest and blend. Add this to the pan and cook for another minute. Add the sugar, 250ml of water and stir until dissolved. Finally add all the remaining ingredients, bring to the boil, then turn down the heat and simmer for roughly 10 minutes, until the mixture starts to thicken slightly.

> **Chef's Tip**
>
> The BBQ sauce recipe will give you plenty left over, so put anything you don't use into sterilised jars and keep in the fridge. It's great with chicken and steaks!

For The Beetroot Slaw

Thinly slice all the vegetables using a sharp knife, and place into a bowl. Add the mayonnaise, then mix in the zest and juice of half a lemon. Season with salt and pepper.

For The Polenta Chips

Simply bring the stock to the boil, whisk in the polenta in a steady stream, bring back to the boil so it's bubbling, then reduce the heat and stir until the mixture thickens. Add the remaining ingredients and give it a good stir, then pour onto a baking sheet lined with clingfilm and spread into a square about 1cm thick. Leave to set.

For The Belly Pork

In the restaurant we *sous-vide* the belly pork by placing in brine first for 12 hours, then vacuum-packing and cooking for 14 hours at 82.5°C in a water bath. If this is not an option, preheat the oven to 200°C. Place the pork in a roasting tin, skin-side up, in the oven for 30 minutes, then reduce the heat to 170°C and cook for a further 2 hours. Baste after the first hour, then again every 30 minutes.

To Serve

Heat a small amount of oil in a frying pan until hot, then add the belly pork and cook for 3-4 minutes until crisp. Turn over and repeat on the other side. Meanwhile, cut the polenta into chips and deep fry until crisp and golden, drain on kitchen paper. Warm the BBQ sauce in a small saucepan then plate as pictured and dress with pea shoots.

PAN ROASTED CORNISH BRILL, HAND-DIVED MUSSELS, SAMPHIRE, PURSLANE & SAFFRON BROTH WITH TEMPURA CORNISH NATIVE OYSTER

SERVES 4

 Camel Valley Bacchus
(Cornwall)

Ingredients

1.2kg brill (filleted and scaled, cut into 4 portions)
4 Cornish native oysters (shucked)
oil (to deep fry)

Broth

1kg hand-dived mussels
1 small red onion
2 cloves garlic
saffron (large pinch of)
50ml white wine
200ml fish stock
1 leek
100g samphire
100g purslane (leaves picked)
50g spinach
parsley (chopped, handful of)

Tempura

100g plain flour
1 tbsp cornflour
½ tsp salt
100-150ml sparkling water (chilled)

Method

For The Tempura

Sieve the flour and cornflour into a bowl and add the salt. Stir until well combined. Whisk enough sparkling water into the flour mixture to form a smooth batter. Heat some oil in a deep pan to 180ºC.

For The Broth

Heat a heavy-bottomed pan and add the mussels, onion, garlic, saffron and white wine. Place a tight fitting lid on and steam until the mussels begin to open. Add the fish stock and bring back to the boil. Simmer for a couple of minutes, then add the vegetables and cook for another 2-3 minutes. Just before serving, mix in the parsley and spinach

For The Brill

While your broth is simmering, place your fish fillets, skin-side down, into a hot frying pan with a little oil. Cook for about 4-5 minutes until you see the flesh changing colour. Flip your fish over and remove the pan from the heat.

> **Chef's Tip**
>
> Dust the skin of the fish with a little flour and seasoning before frying to get a crispy, golden brown finish.

To Serve

Dip your oysters into flour, then the tempura batter and deep fry in the hot oil. Once the oyster is crisp, remove and drain on kitchen paper. Divide your broth between 4 serving bowls, top with the brill then the oyster and a squeeze of lemon juice.

CHOCOLATE, CARAMEL & PEANUT TORTE, EARL GREY BANANAS WITH VANILLA ICE CREAM

SERVES 4

Dulce de Pasas, Toro Albala
(Spain)

Ingredients

Caramel

60g butter
40g brown sugar
15ml honey
200ml condensed milk
100g peanuts (crushed)

Torte

150g chocolate biscuits
25g butter (melted)
85g chocolate (at least 65% cocoa)
1 tbsp golden syrup
150ml double cream

Earl Grey Bananas

2 bananas
70g caster sugar
25ml liquid glucose
1 Earl Grey tea bag
15ml dark rum
1 lemon (zest and juice of)

Ice Cream

500ml double cream
1 vanilla pod (split lengthways)
50g caster sugar
75ml water
2 egg yolks (beaten)

Garnish

peanuts (crushed)

4 x 70mm metal rings

Chef's Tip

Use a blow torch to warm the metal rings, making it easier to remove the tortes and use it to give the tortes a quick glaze.

Method

For The Caramel

Put all the ingredients, excluding the peanuts, into a pan and bring slowly to the boil, stirring constantly. Cook for a few minutes then remove from the heat. Stir in the peanuts and set to one side.

For The Torte

Place 4 metal rings onto a baking sheet lined with baking parchment. Crush the chocolate biscuits in a food processor or with a rolling pin, then mix in the melted butter. Divide between the 4 rings and press firmly down. Top with the caramel, and pop in the fridge.

Melt the chocolate, golden syrup and 50ml of the cream over a pan of simmering water. When melted, remove from the heat. Whip the remaining cream to soft peaks and fold into the chocolate. Divide the mix between the 4 rings and place back into the fridge to set.

For The Bananas

Melt the sugar and glucose over a low heat, then turn the heat up and boil the sugar until it starts to turn caramel in colour. Add the rum and 5ml of lemon juice, then boil until it reaches a liquid consistency. Remove from the heat and add the lemon zest. Cool for roughly 10 minutes.

Peel the bananas and place into a vacuum bag with the caramel and teabag. Seal on a medium vacuum. Cook the bananas in a water bath at 65ºC for 45 minutes. Remove and leave the bananas to cool in the caramel. If you do not have a water bath simply toss the bananas through the caramel when removed from the heat and leave to cool. Omit the Earl Grey tea bag.

For The Ice Cream

Bring the cream almost to boiling point, remove from the heat and add the vanilla pod. Leave to infuse until the cream is cold. Scrape out the pod and leave the seeds in the cream.

Dissolve the sugar in the water over a low heat, then turn up the heat and boil to produce a light syrup. Leave the mixture to cool for just 1 minute.

Place the egg yolks in a bowl and trickle in the hot syrup a little at a time. Whisk until the mixture is thick, then whisk in the cream. Pour into an ice cream machine and churn until frozen, or see page 231.

To Serve

Arrange as pictured.

190
SECOND FLOOR
RESTAURANT & BAR

Harvey Nichols, 27 Philadelphia Street, Cabot Circus, Bristol, BS1 3BZ

01179 168 898
www.harveynichols.com

Beyond the designer dresses and sharp suits of the Harvey Nichols' shop floor in the heart of Bristol city centre, lies one of Bristol's finest restaurants. The Second Floor Restaurant and Bar brings the Harvey Nichols luxury and fashion experience to the south west.

Renowned as one of the premium restaurants in the south west, The Second Floor Restaurant and Bar offers the very best in modern cooking. Award-winning executive chef Louise McCrimmon uses the freshest seasonal ingredients to create an exciting selection of all day dining menus, from brunch right through to dinner. Each dish expertly combines classic techniques and indulgent tastes for seasonally changing specialities.

The Second Floor Restaurant boasts a winning combination of modern British cooking and the best ingredients the south west has to offer. Decorated in decadent gold, the stylish setting and impressive menu has won a legion of fans, from national food critics to the city's trend-setters.

With opulent sofas, sumptuously-upholstered fawn leather chairs and a fabulous wall of wine, Second Floor Restaurant is a temple to fashion and gastronomy. Vast plate glass windows provide commanding views across Quaker's Friars and other parts of the city.

The 60-seat room has become a place in which to see and be seen. Offering all day dining from breakfast, lunch to indulgent afternoon teas and sumptuous evening menus, diners can relax in plenty of space among the business classes, fashionistas, ladies who lunch and guests from throughout the south west.

Relish Restaurant Rewards
See page 003 for details.

Executive chef Louise McCrimmon trained under
Prue Leith at Leiths School of Food and Wine.
She was asked to launch the new Harvey Nichols
restaurant in Bristol five years ago, but she loved it
so much that she stayed.

"The south west has a very relaxed ambience with
plenty of exceptional suppliers. I work with a great
team and fabulous produce - what more could you
ask for?"

SEARED PIGEON BREAST, MOROCCAN SPICED DUCK PASTILLA, CARROT & HARISSA PUREE, YOGHURT & LEMON

SERVES 4

 Decenio Rioja Reserva, 2001 (Spain)

Ingredients

2 pigeon breasts

Duck Leg Pastilla

2 duck legs
1 tsp coriander seeds
1 tsp cardamom pods
cinnamon stick (2cm piece)
1 tsp cumin seeds
2 strips orange zest
3 cloves garlic (peeled)
½ tsp fennel seeds
50g rock salt
500g duck fat
½ packet filo pastry
25g currants
25g pistachios
1 tbsp coriander (freshly chopped)
1 tbsp mint (freshly chopped)
10g sesame seeds

Carrot Purée

250g carrots
2 tsp rose harissa

Yoghurt

200g Greek yoghurt
salt and pepper

1 preserved lemon (flesh removed, skin finely diced)

Method

For The Duck Pastilla

Blitz all the dry spices, garlic, orange zest and salt together and sprinkle over the duck legs. Leave for 24 hours, then rinse. Melt the duck fat and completely cover the duck legs. Cook slowly at 140°C for 1½ hours until tender. Cool slightly, pick the duck meat and shred. Mix with the currants and pistachios and finally with the freshly chopped coriander and mint.

Cut the filo pastry into rectangles and brush with melted butter. Place 3 sheets on top of each other, place the duck filling at one end and roll up to make a cigar shape. Brush with melted butter and sprinkle with sesame seeds. Bake for 12 minutes at 180°C until golden.

For The Carrot Purée

Peel and slice the carrots evenly. Steam until tender. Purée until really smooth and add rose harissa to taste.

For The Yoghurt (Prepare the day before)

Line a sieve with a clean cloth and place over a jug. Season the yoghurt with salt and pepper, place in the sieve and leave to hang over the jug overnight, until thick.

To Serve

Sear the pigeon breasts, skin-side down, in a hot pan and cook in a mixture of olive oil and butter. Do not overcook.

Allow to rest for 5 minutes, and then carve the pigeon in half. Season with rock salt. Serve with carrot purée, a *quenelle* of the yoghurt topped with preserved lemon and the duck pastilla.

WILD RABBIT SADDLE, RABBIT & LEEK PIE, SWEETCORN PUREE, CHANTENAY CARROTS, RABBIT JUS

SERVES 4

🍷 *Harvey Nichols Barbera d'Asti, Marchesi di Grésy 2009, Piedmont (Italy)*

Ingredients

2 wild rabbits (legs removed, loins taken from the saddle)
4 slices Parma ham
25g butter
salt and pepper (to season)

Rabbit Pie Filling

10ml olive oil
4 rabbit legs (floured and seasoned)
1 large onion (chopped)
1 clove garlic
small bunch thyme
small bunch tarragon
1 litre chicken stock
100ml double cream
1 leek (chopped)

Pastry

400g flour
½ tsp salt
250g cold butter
140ml water (cold)
egg yolk (to glaze)

Sweetcorn Purée

2 corn on the cobs
25g butter
salt and pepper (to season)
100ml chicken stock (if required)

Carrots

chantenay carrots
50g butter
water (to cover)

Garnish

rabbit *jus*

4 x 6cm pie rings (greased)

Method

For The Saddles

Take the loins off the rabbit saddle and remove all silver sinew. Spread the two rabbit loins with butter and sandwich together. Wrap in Parma ham. Roll tightly in several layers of clingfilm to form a cylinder. Chill.

For The Filling

Heat the olive oil in a large sauté pan and lightly colour the floured and seasoned legs on all sides then remove. Gently sweat the onion for 4-5 minutes. Add the garlic, thyme and rabbit legs. Add the stock, bring to the boil, then simmer for 40 minutes or until tender. Remove the legs and allow to cool. When cool, pick the meat from the bones into bite size pieces.

Strain the liquid. Bring to the boil and reduce by half. Add the cream and boil for another 15 minutes until you have a smooth sauce. Check the seasoning.

Sweat the leeks until just soft, mix with the rabbit pieces, tarragon and sauce. Check the seasoning. Allow to chill before using.

For The Pastry

Rub the cold butter into the dry ingredients. Add the water and combine. Do not overwork. Chill and rest in the fridge for 30 minutes. Roll out to 3mm thick, line the pie rings and cut out circles to top the pie. Chill for 15 minutes.

To Assemble The Pie

Fill the pie rings with the rabbit mixture, cover with the pastry lid and crimp the edges. Make a slit in the top to allow steam to escape. Glaze with egg yolk. Bake for 20 minutes at 180°C until crisp and golden.

For The Sweetcorn Purée

Cook the sweetcorn in boiling salted water until tender. Cut the corn kernels off the cob and purée with butter, seasoning and a little stock if necessary. Pass through a sieve, removing all skin, so that you get a silky smooth purée.

For The Carrots

Cook the carrots in the butter and enough water to cover.

To Serve

Warm the purée. Poach the rabbit loin in barely simmering water for 10 minutes. Unwrap and sear in butter and oil until golden. Leave to rest for at least 5 minutes. To assemble, slice the rabbit loin and serve with the sweetcorn purée, chantenay carrots, pie and rabbit *jus*.

PASSION FRUIT CANNELLONI, LEMONGRASS ICE CREAM & PASSION FRUIT CURD

SERVES 6

Seifried Sweet Agnes Riesling, Nelson, 2012
(New Zealand)

Ingredients

For The Passion Fruit Curd

5 passion fruits
1 large egg
1 large egg yolk
75g caster sugar
75g unsalted butter

Passion Fruit Jelly

110ml passion fruit purée
50g sugar
1.75g agar agar
1 leaf gelatine (soaked in water)
11ml water

For The Coconut Mousse

3 leaves gelatine (soaked in water)
80g sugar
250g coconut purée
250ml double cream (lightly whipped)

For The Lemongrass Ice Cream

200ml double cream
300ml full-fat milk
4 sticks lemongrass
3 egg yolks
100g caster sugar
2 tbsp liquid glucose

Tuile Biscuit

125g butter (melted, cooled)
125g sugar
4 egg whites
125g plain flour
20g desiccated coconut

Method

For The Passion Fruit Curd
Put the seeded pulp of the passion fruit into a processor and blitz just to loosen the seeds. Strain into a jug or bowl. Beat the egg, egg yolk and sugar together. Melt the butter over a low heat in a heavy-bottomed pan, and, when melted, stir in the sugar and egg mixture and the passion fruit juice. Keep cooking gently, stirring constantly, until thickened. Cool and refrigerate.

For the Passion Fruit Jelly
Mix the sugar and agar agar. Boil the passion fruit purée, add the agar agar and sugar mixture and cook for 3-4 minutes. The agar must dissolve. Add the gelatine, stir to dissolve and pass through a *chinois*. Pour onto a lightly greased shallow tray measuring 24cm x 30cm then cool.

For The Coconut Mousse
Using Cellophane, make 2 tubes, 18cm long, and the diameter of a £2 coin. Use Sellotape to secure them and clingfilm one end.

Add the sugar to the purée and warm to dissolve. Add the gelatine, dissolve and pass through a fine sieve. Cool, and when beginning to set, fold in the lightly whipped cream. Put into a piping bag, pipe into the tubes and chill.

To Assemble
Trim the jelly into 4 x 6x30cm wide rectangles whilst in the tray. Unwrap the coconut mousse and cut into 6cm lengths (3 pieces per 18cm tube). Place onto a portion of the jelly and roll up, as pictured.

For The Ice Cream
Bruise the lemongrass and add it to the milk and cream. Bring to the boil, remove from the heat and leave to infuse for 2 hours. Whisk the eggs and sugar together until thick. Bring the milk mixture back to the boil and pour onto the egg and sugar mixture. Add the liquid glucose and cook out until thickened, stirring frequently. Pass through a fine sieve and chill. Churn in an ice cream machine, or see page 231.

For The Tuile Biscuit
Preheat the oven to 160ºC.

Whisk the egg whites until they start to go frothy, then add the sugar and whisk until glossy. Add the melted butter whilst slowly whisking the egg whites, then the flour until all blended.

Put in a piping bag and pipe 14cm lengths onto a tray lined with greased greaseproof paper.

Sprinkle with desiccated coconut and bake for 5-7 minutes. While they are still warm, wrap around a metal cylinder to form spirals.

To Serve
Serve dish as pictured.

200
THE THREE GABLES

1 St Margaret's Street, Bradford-on-Avon, Wiltshire, BA15 1DA

01225 781 666
www.thethreegables.com

Customers know they are in safe hands when they plan a trip to The Three Gables, in picturesque Bradford-on-Avon. The old stone building, which dates back more than 350 years, is run by two of the best-known and most talented operators in the south west.

Restaurant manager Vito Scaduto and classically-trained chef Marc Salmon each have more than two decades experience in the region's finest restaurants and hotels. They decided to open The Three Gables two years ago, after the property had stood empty for more than 20 years. A year was spent transforming the venue into a temple for exceptional regional food, which is much loved by discerning diners from across the region.

"The Three Gables is a truly wonderful building," said Vito. "We wanted to respect its traditions, but also create a light and contemporary dining space for our guests." The duo's delightful, independently run restaurant has been sensitively restored, with many of the original timbers and stonework being lovingly revealed, making for a truly beautiful refurbishment.

Since its opening in 2011, this establishment has become a popular dining destination, known for its quality food, superb wines and the warm welcome provided by Vito and his team. Its ground floor lounge bar provides the perfect place in which to relax while the first floor restaurant provides unrivalled views across the river Avon and Bradford's famous bridge.

Relish Restaurant Rewards
See page 003 for details.

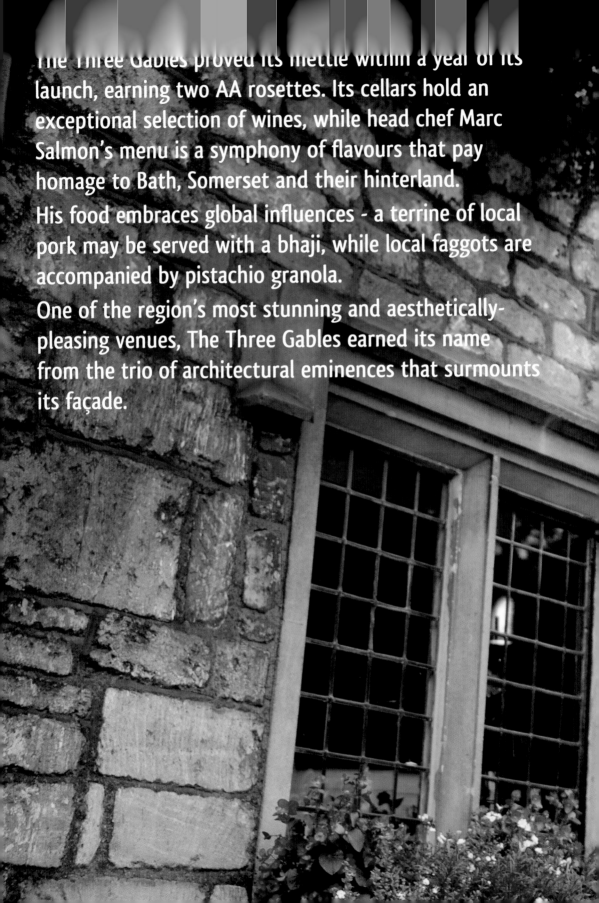

The Three Gables proved its mettle within a year of its launch, earning two AA rosettes. Its cellars hold an exceptional selection of wines, while head chef Marc Salmon's menu is a symphony of flavours that pay homage to Bath, Somerset and their hinterland.

His food embraces global influences - a terrine of local pork may be served with a bhaji, while local faggots are accompanied by pistachio granola.

One of the region's most stunning and aesthetically-pleasing venues, The Three Gables earned its name from the trio of architectural eminences that surmounts its façade.

TRUFFLED FARLEIGH WALLOP FRITTER, PICKLED GIROLLES, BEETROOT RELISH & THYME CRACKERS

SERVES 6

 Soave Classico DOC 2010 Pieropan (Italy)

Ingredients

Pickled Girolle Mushrooms

100g girolle mushrooms (trimmed and washed)
300ml white wine vinegar
100ml water
100ml white wine
200g caster sugar
2 tbsp pickling spice

Beetroot Relish

400g beetroot (peeled and grated)
1 red onion (finely chopped)
2 tbsp olive oil
50g soft brown sugar
100ml red wine vinegar
100ml red wine
1 tbsp mustard seeds

Thyme Crackers

30g butter (cold, diced)
120g plain flour
1 tsp baking powder
6 sprigs thyme (finely chopped)
salt (pinch of)
50 ml water

Farleigh Wallop Fritter

2 Farleigh Wallop goat's cheeses (or any kind of soft goat's cheese - rind removed, grated)
truffle oil (drizzle of)
1 small truffle (optional)
100g plain flour
2 eggs (beaten)
200g Panko breadcrumbs

Garnish

micro herbs (celery, mustard frill)

Method

For The Pickled Mushrooms

Place the mushrooms in a bowl. Put all the other ingredients into a saucepan and bring to the boil, then leave to cool. Bring back to the boil and strain over the mushrooms. Cover the bowl with clingfilm and leave to cool.

Chef's Tip

You can prepare the pickled girolle mushrooms well in advance as they will keep for several days in the fridge.

For The Beetroot Relish

Sweat the onion and beetroot with the olive oil in a saucepan for 5 minutes. Add the rest of the ingredients, bring to the boil, mix well, lower the heat and continue to cook until a jam-like consistency is achieved (after approximately 30 minutes). The relish can also be prepared well in advance. Store in a sterilised jar.

For The Thyme Crackers

Place everything except the water in a food processor and blitz for 1 minute. Add the water and blitz again until a smooth dough is formed. Roll the dough as thinly as possible between 2 sheets of greaseproof paper and chill for 1 hour. Cut out with a cutter of your choice. Place the crackers on a baking tray and bake at 180°C for about 10 minutes or until golden.

For The Farleigh Wallop Fritters

Thoroughly mix the goat's cheese, truffle and truffle oil. Roll the mixture in clingfilm into a 3cm cylinder and place into the freezer for 2 hours. Take out of the freezer, remove the clingfilm and cut into 6 portions. Carefully roll the portions in flour, followed by the beaten egg and finally the breadcrumbs. Deep fry for approximately 1-2 minutes until golden. Remove and drain on kitchen paper.

To Serve

Arrange as pictured and garnish with some micro herbs, such as celery and mustard frill.

FILLET OF BEEF, BONE MARROW POLENTA & HERITAGE CARROTS

SERVES 6

*Cantemerle 2000 Haut-Médoc
(France)*

Ingredients

6 x 200g beef fillet steaks (centre cut)

Bone Marrow Polenta

2 bone marrows (split)
100g polenta
50g Parmesan (grated)
300ml water
100ml double cream
salt and pepper (pinch of)

Parsley Purée

2 bunches curly-leaf parsley (washed)
salt and pepper (pinch of)

Carrot Syrup

400g carrots (peeled and trimmed)

Heritage Carrots

8 medium-sized heritage carrots
(2 orange, 2 yellow, 2 purple, 2 white - peeled)
butter (knob of)

Red Wine Jus

250ml red wine
500ml beef stock

Garnish

baby Lilliput capers

Method

For The Bone Marrow Polenta

Preheat the oven to 220°C. Roast the marrow bones for 10 minutes, allow to cool, and scrape out the marrow into a saucepan. Add the remaining ingredients. Slowly bring to the boil, whisking all the time. Continue to cook for 5-10 minutes over a low heat and mix well with a spatula until it's thick and smooth. Spread the mix onto a non-stick tray keeping a 1cm thickness, allow to cool, cut into 3cm squares, then cut diagonally. Panfry the pieces of polenta for 2 minutes on either side, remove, drain on kitchen paper and keep warm.

For The Parsley Purée

De-stalk the parsley. Cook the stalks in boiling salted water for 5 minutes, add the parsley leaves and boil for a further 5 minutes. Drain in a colander, then blitz in a blender until smooth. Season with a little salt and pepper.

For The Carrot Syrup

Juice the carrots in a juice extractor. Reduce the carrot juice in a saucepan until it's thick and syrupy.

For The Heritage Carrots

Cut the carrots into 2cm wedges and cook separately in boiling salted water until just done, or *al dente*. Drain and gently panfry in butter until golden. Season and keep warm.

For The Red Wine Jus

Add the red wine and beef stock to a pan, bring to the boil, then turn down the heat slightly. Reduce until it thickens and the flavour is concentrated.

For The Beef Fillet

Season the steaks well with salt and pepper. Seal in a hot frying pan, lower the heat, and continue to cook for 2 minutes on either side. Remove from the pan and allow to rest for 5 minutes.

To Serve

Smear some parsley purée onto a warm plate, arrange the polenta and carrots on top. Carve the steaks and arrange on the plate, drizzle with some carrot syrup, sprinkle with the baby capers and serve with some red wine *jus* on the side.

WHITE CHOCOLATE & AMARENA CHERRY PARFAIT, DARK CHOCOLATE MOUSSE, CHERRY SORBET

SERVES 6

🍷 *De Bortoli Noble One Botrytis Semillon 2008*
(Australia)

Ingredients

Dark Chocolate Mousse

150g good quality dark chocolate (melted)
3 egg yolks
120g caster sugar
50ml water
300ml double cream (semi-whipped)

White Chocolate And Amarena Cherry Parfait

150g good quality white chocolate (melted)
3 egg yolks
120g caster sugar
50ml water
300ml double cream (semi-whipped)
20 Amarena cherries (drained, chopped)
2 thin sheets plain sponge cake
100g cherry jam

Cherry Sorbet

400g fresh cherries (pitted) or frozen cherry purée
250ml water
200g caster sugar

Garnish

12 Amarena cherries
Amarena cherry syrup
chocolate

Method

For The Dark Chocolate Mousse

Whisk the egg yolks on high speed in a mixing machine. Boil the sugar with the water in a saucepan until a thick syrup is achieved (or the soft ball stage, 110-115ºC, if using a sugar thermometer). Gently pour the hot syrup onto the whisking egg yolks and continue to whisk for a further 10 minutes. Remove the whisk, fold in the melted chocolate, then fold in the semi-whipped cream. Place the mousse in a bowl and refrigerate.

For The White Chocolate And Amarena Parfait

Repeat the process used for the dark chocolate mousse, but use white chocolate instead. Once you have folded in the whipped cream, fold in the chopped cherries, then roll the mix in clingfilm into 2cm cylinders and freeze for 3 hours. Spread the cherry jam onto the sponge sheets. Unwrap the frozen parfait cylinders and place on the sponge sheets. Roll up until completely covered and re-freeze.

For The Frozen Cherry Sorbet

Place all the ingredients into a saucepan and bring to the boil. Add to a blender then blitz until smooth. Strain through a fine sieve, leave to cool then churn in an ice cream maker, or see page 231. Freeze until needed.

To Serve

Remove the parfait from the freezer and slice into 2cm slices, making 3 slices per portion. Place on a plate and leave to defrost slightly, for approximately 5 minutes. Place the dark chocolate mousse into a piping bag and pipe onto the plates between the slices of parfait as pictured. Place a scoop of cherry sorbet onto one of the parfait slices and garnish with the cherries, syrup and chocolate decorations.

210
THE TOWER INN

Church Road, Slapton, Kingsbridge, Devon, TQ7 2PN

01548 580 216
www.thetowerinn.com

The Tower Inn is hidden in the shadow of the 14th Century tower it stands beside. Tucked away in Slapton village, nestling beside a national nature reserve, the pub is a haven for lovers of great food and drink in a beautiful setting. For the past seven years we have worked hard to build an outstanding reputation for food, enjoyed in an historic building with an informal, relaxed atmosphere.

Our food is all about local, seasonal produce and many of our suppliers are subsequently great friends of ours. We aim to put a twist on traditional pub classics, but can't deny the influence of our head chef Dom, who stems from Lyon, France. Having worked with many top chefs over the years, such as Jean-Christophe Novelli and Pierre Chevillard, Dom brings over 35 years of experience and knowledge.

Whether it is summer or winter, the pub always offers the perfect hideaway to sit back, relax and enjoy our family welcome.

Relish Restaurant Rewards
See page 003 for details.